PENGUIN BOOKS

THE PENGUIN CLASSICS
CROSSWORD PUZZLES

Ben Tausig began creating crosswords in 2004 and published his first puzzles in *USA Today* and the *Los Angeles Times* at the end of that year. In early 2005, he published his first of many puzzles in the *New York Times* and simultaneously began syndicating a weekly puzzle feature called Ink Well to alternative newspapers throughout North America, including the *Village Voice*, *San Francisco Bay Guardian*, *Chicago Reader*, *Toronto Eye Weekly*, and *Washington City Paper*. He later also became editor of *The Onion* A.V. Club crossword, a feature that continues to appear weekly in *The Onion* nationwide. He enjoys running, watching baseball, and cooking with his wife.

D0846253

The
PENGUIN CLASSICS
CROSSWORD PUZZLES

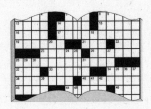

Edited by

Ben Tausig

PENGUIN BOOKS

PENGUIN BOOKS

Published by the Penguin Group

Penguin Group (USA) Inc., 375 Hudson Street, New York, New York 10014, U.S.A.

Penguin Group (Canada), 90 Eglinton Avenue East, Suite 700, Toronto, Ontario, Canada M4P 2Y3
(a division of Pearson Penguin Canada Inc.)

Penguin Books Ltd, 80 Strand, London WC2R 0RL, England

Penguin Ireland, 25 St Stephen's Green, Dublin 2, Ireland (a division of Penguin Books Ltd)

Penguin Group (Australia), 250 Camberwell Road, Camberwell, Victoria 3124, Australia
(a division of Pearson Australia Group Pty Ltd)

Penguin Books India Pvt Ltd, 11 Community Centre, Panchsheel Park, New Delhi – 110 017, India

Penguin Group (NZ), 67 Apollo Drive, Rosedale, Auckland 0632, New Zealand
(a division of Pearson New Zealand Ltd)

Penguin Books (South Africa) (Pty) Ltd, 24 Sturdee Avenue, Rosebank, Johannesburg 2196,
South Africa

Penguin Books Ltd, Registered Offices:
80 Strand, London WC2R 0RL, England

First published in Penguin Books 2011

10 9 8 7 6 5 4 3

ISBN 978-0-14-311980-7
CIP data available

Printed in the United States of America
Set in Chaparral Pro
Designed by Sabrina Bowers

For Serena, who helps

CROSSWORDS

1

ACROSS

1. Chain hotel, for short
5. Extreme Texas Hold 'Em bet
10. Composer Stravinsky
14. Member of a '70s R&B group
15. Raccoon relative
16. Drop, from a manuscript
17. Dickensian waif served with onions?
19. Reasons to visit a clinic: Abbr.
20. Mediterranean tourist city
21. Baum barker
23. "Iliad" character?
24. Nor. neighbor
25. Write (down)
28. Cordelia's father listening attentively?
30. "The War of the Worlds" base
32. Call, as a basketball game
34. Bias
35. Stake
37. Butting heads
38. Flaubert's heroine embracing motherhood?
40. Anticipate
42. Big name in early video games
43. Construction site sight, familiarly
44. Relatives
45. Smartphone programs, for short
49. Shakespearean fairy after doing sit-ups?
52. Cardinal letters?
54. Coastline feature
55. ___ canto
56. J. M. Barrie pirate
58. O. Henry device
60. Bass colleague
62. Sewell's horse with a lovely saddle?
65. Blockhead
66. Young Jetson
67. "Aha!"
68. Eat
69. Be green, in a way
70. Correspondent's output: Abbr.

DOWN

1. "Total patient" philosophy
2. The Chippewa, by another name
3. Bardem of "No Country for Old Men"
4. Court attention-getter
5. Play a part
6. Burner setting
7. Café au ___
8. "There, there"
9. Capone crony
10. They may be checked at the door
11. "Here it comes!"
12. Seasoned pro
13. Getaway spots
18. Paul Scott's "The ___ Quartet"
22. GM roadside help service
26. Calliope's cousin
27. Abound
29. "All in the Family" role
31. River in a Stephen Foster song
33. Flip (out)
36. Prettifies
37. ___-garde
38. "Congratulations on your Bar Mitzvah!"
39. "Miss ___ Regrets"
40. "Fanfare for the Common Cold" composer
41. Erstwhile gossip columnist Parsons
46. "Swann's Way" author
47. "The Birthday Party" playwright Harold
48. Confirm an engagement?
50. Hardened sap
51. Memphis "blues" street
53. Bit of deception
57. Stocking color
59. Commuter line, perhaps
61. Keats's "___ to a Grecian Urn"
63. Dramatic ends to boxing matches, for short
64. "Until we meet again . . ."

Body of Literature

TONY ORBACH AND AMY REYNALDO

2

ACROSS

1. Without financial means
5. Bros
10. Whim
14. Overhang
15. Sphinx country
16. ____ Go Bragh
17. Seize
18. Disgraced journalist Jayson
19. Source of some modern therapy
20. Alcohol, for some
23. Place to get stuck
24. In favor of
25. 16th-century violin maker
28. Driver Foyt and pitcher Burnett
31. Dynamite inventor
35. Creative region
38. Sanitary pad option
39. Tribute
40. Grocery store freebies
42. "___ Just Not That Into You"
43. Without
45. Sensation of sorrow
47. First name in cosmetics
49. Hereditary material
50. Leaves
51. In the manner of
53. Visitor center offering
54. Character who promises each of the second words in 20-, 35-, and 45-Across
61. Arms or drag follower
62. WWII sub
63. Appear
66. Plant that may be used to treat burns
67. Cool, after not being cool for awhile
68. Therefore
69. Lilypad locale
70. Old-time anesthetic
71. Hit video game introduced in 1993

DOWN

1. 1977 Steely Dan hit
2. Rower's need
3. Track shape
4. Renaissance
5. First performance
6. Citrus also called "Uniq Fruit"
7. Twosome
8. Long and involved
9. Old-timey barber's tool
10. First-class perk
11. ___ code
12. Engagement jewelry
13. Body part with a cap
21. Cedes the game
22. Tea water dispenser, perhaps
25. Left the couch
26. Greedy king of myth
27. Hollywood representer
28. Packing heat
29. Country with a city named Obama
30. Brazilian president Luiz Inácio da ___
32. Faith founded in Persia
33. Put forth
34. Things may be ticked off from them
36. Scrooge's cry
37. Marshal under Napoleon
41. Bundle, as of papers
44. Nori, e.g.
46. Naked
48. Yale student
52. Sky blue
53. Travel by car
54. "It's a ___!"
55. Radiant ring
56. Paul Krugman's subj.
57. Drive the getaway car, say
58. "The Plot Against America" novelist Philip
59. Oft-criticized anti-drug program for youth
60. Round number?
64. Self-esteem
65. Pop's counterpart

If Only

JOHN CUNNINGHAM

1	2	3	4		5	6	7	8	9		10	11	12	13
14					15						16			
17					18						19			
		20		21						22				
		23						24						
25	26	27				28	29	30		31		32	33	34
35					36				37		38			
39				40					41			42		
43			44		45						46			
47				48		49				50				
		51		52				53						
54	55	56				57	58	59				60		
61					62						63		64	65
66					67						68			
69					70						71			

3

ACROSS

1. Big celebration
5. Get ready to eat?
10. Equestrian pace
14. Cinematic partner of Stitch
15. Come up
16. Suffix with zillion
17. River to the Baltic
18. SPOILER ALERT! . . . He dies after renouncing chivalry
20. "Boom! Like that . . ."
22. "Come here ___?" (boring pickup line)
23. "Star Trek: T.N.G." counselor Deanna
24. In other words
26. SPOILER ALERT! . . . He gets assassinated in Act III
30. Parody paper, with "The"
31. Superfecta, e.g.
32. Island visited by "The Stranger" in a 1990s video game
36. Lbs. and ozs., e.g.
37. Where some ideas look good
41. H, to Hera
42. Shape for some meat
44. Projectile's path
45. Perfume ingredient
47. SPOILER ALERT! . . . She throws herself in front of a train
51. Maximize an opportunity
54. Prefix with conference, photo, or vision
55. Star-reader Sydney
56. Avenges
60. SPOILER ALERT! . . . He dies after stabbing a painting
63. Common basketball defense
64. Big name in Art Deco design
65. Nicely baked, say
66. Write with acid
67. Marine meal
68. Zellweger who plays Bridget
69. Supermarket section

DOWN

1. Classic sci-fi creature, with "The"
2. Operatic Ethiopian princess
3. Musher's conveyance
4. Hamlet's confidante
5. Signals for help from a ship, perhaps
6. Alanis Morissette hit that irked some linguists
7. Bad engine sound
8. Abbr. on a lawyer's letterhead
9. Recent, in the Rhineland
10. W-9 or 1099, e.g.
11. Mob scenes
12. "Coffee ___?" (host's offering)
13. Little
19. Little bit
21. Sacha Baron Cohen character
24. Trickle
25. Bone: Prefix
26. Bloodhound's sine qua non
27. Golden Rule preposition
28. Ms. Kudrow
29. One way to be taken
33. Himalayan legend
34. British submachine gun
35. "Gone With the Wind" setting
38. "Peter Pan" pooch
39. Word in a 2006 Elizabeth Gilbert title
40. Projection units
43. Spenser's spirits
46. Reacted to pepper, perhaps
48. Drag racing org.
49. "Chill," on the base
50. Confirm, as a password
51. Old PC accessory
52. Dean Martin's "That's ___"
53. Small-scale racers
56. Emulate the Cheshire Cat
57. Exercise the franchise
58. Ltr. insert
59. Classic soda brand
61. Big name in ATMs
62. Test for some college srs.

Spoiler Alert

SAM DONALDSON

4

ACROSS

1. Declines
5. Organic fertilizer
10. Combustible heap
14. Nonclerical
15. ___ Gay (fateful WWII bomber)
16. Summer month along the Seine
17. Sicilian mount
18. Like steno pads
19. Crazy
20. Where to read about Wilbur and Templeton
23. Business card abbr. next to a 10-digit number
24. Sue Grafton's "___ for Alibi"
25. Venomous snakes
28. Fire starter?
29. Some NCOs
31. Shirt or blouse
32. With "The," where to read about Baloo and Kaa
36. Prefix with -gon
37. The end of ___
38. ___-Locka, Florida
39. Small, silver salmon
40. Mitts
41. Where to read about Napoleon and Boxer
43. "The ___-King" (Goethe poem)
44. "Back ____ hour"
45. Showy moths
46. Atlanta suburb
48. MGM motto word
49. "Survivor" station
52. Where to read about Piglet and Kanga
56. Capital on the Dnieper River
58. Halved
59. Something that may come to a head?
60. Shoppe sign word
61. "___ is born"
62. Workplace benefit
63. Fly or gnat, e.g.
64. Back at sea?
65. Gaelic tongue

DOWN

1. Put in office
2. Use the tub, say
3. Double
4. "The Lion King" villain
5. "Helpful" hinter
6. Pieces of product
7. ___ Blanc
8. Peter Fonda title role
9. Perennial loser
10. Like windows
11. "Sure thing!"
12. Non-groovy groove?
13. GRE org.
21. Ms. Ali in the ring
22. Dict. entries
26. Helicopter mechanism
27. Sudden burst of activity
28. Baseball VIPs
29. Stop by
30. Head at the bar
32. Pulls someone's leg, say
33. Take pieces from?
34. Recently licensed couple
35. ___ fide
36. Sounds elicited by pows
39. End
41. Biblical liar
42. World Cup noisemaker
44. Place to stop and rest
47. Hold the attention of
48. Doing battle
49. Certain computer program creator
50. Some South Africans
51. Prepare, as a can of shaving cream
53. Brief moment: Abbr.
54. Kitchen extension?
55. Water carrier
56. Keystone character
57. Martinique, e.g.

Classical Creatures

SARAH KELLER

5

ACROSS

1. Henry's pupil
6. Hero who wooed and then jilted Medea
11. "Hey, it's a ___"
14. Painter of Rouen cathedral, many times
15. Scene of activity
16. Prefix with skeleton
17. 1874 novel subtitled "A Study of Provincial Life"
19. Stout of crime fiction
20. "___ you crazy?!?"
21. Antarctic penguin
22. Fashion label letters
23. Certain bigots
25. Stitch (up)
26. 2008 James Bond novel by Sebastian Faulks writing as Ian Fleming
32. Peace amidst chaos, metaphorically
35. Person who's well-connected?
36. Transfixed
37. Non-bidder's declaration, in bridge
39. Captain of the Nautilus
40. Test performance
42. Others: Sp.
43. 1986 book adapted from the diary of Anaïs Nin
46. Fair-hiring abbr.
47. Suffered humiliation
51. Uncontrolled
53. Act divisions
56. Former Soviet space station
57. Big diamond?
58. 1982 Nadine Gordimer novel
60. Marks, as a ballot
61. Love, Italian-style
62. Vichyssoise vegetables
63. Gridiron gains: Abbr.
64. Namesake of Wednesday
65. "Would you like ___ with that?"

DOWN

1. Title heroines for Austen and Flaubert
2. France's longest river
3. Dow Jones, e.g.
4. Last letter, in Canada
5. They can show you the world
6. Probable dedicatee of "Macbeth" and descendant of the historical Banquo
7. Shrinking Asian sea
8. World Golf Hall of Famer Pak
9. Not again?
10. Informal refusal
11. Insignificant, as a town
12. Farm team?
13. Like the Honda Element
18. 1999 Ron Howard film
22. Prepared to serve, as red wine
24. Annual Anchorage-to-Nome race
25. Isr. neighbor
27. "___ behold!"
28. House of Commons reps
29. Two-time loser to DDE
30. Tomato variety
31. Son of Aphrodite and Ares (according to some)
32. Straight: Prefix
33. River through Bern
34. Cowardly
37. "Rosemary's Baby" author Levin
38. "Atheism is a non-prophet organization," e.g.
41. Corrosive hydroxide
42. "To love ___ is the beginning of a lifelong romance": Oscar Wilde
44. 1994 Olympic speed skater Dan
45. Sch. near the Rio Grande
48. Architect of the National Gallery of Art's East Building
49. "Duino Elegies" poet Rainer Maria
50. Head lock?
51. Like Stilton cheese
52. Like ready champagne
53. Competition for true heavyweights
54. Lummox

Book of the Month

JOON PAHK

55. Rochester's love
58. Trash-talk, with "at"
59. Not neath

6

ACROSS

1. To's opposite
4. Desert prickers
9. Sound represented by an upside-down e
14. Young man
15. Nasal spray brand
16. Acrylic fiber
17. Affirmative on deck
18. Areas in Clue
19. Renowned
20. Bertolt Brecht's profiteer
23. Follow logically
24. Author Capote, to friends
25. Org. with many guards
28. Short story by George Eliot
33. "I wandered lonely ___ cloud": Wordsworth
36. "Swann's ___" (Marcel Proust work)
37. Welcome to one's home
38. What Othello fears he has become
41. Take part in a tournament
43. Moving about
44. "Ode ___ Nightingale"
45. "Neither a borrower ___ a lender be"
46. Theodore Dreiser novel
51. Formula One racer Fabi
52. Matterhorn, e.g.
53. Release
57. Lewis Carroll parody
62. John Fowles novel, with "The"
64. Rolls partner in automobiles
65. Poe's "The Murders in the ___ Morgue"
66. Public forum of ancient Greece
67. Tropical nuts
68. Horton the elephant sat on one
69. Wood that repels moths
70. Refine, as metal
71. Jean Rhys's "Wide Sargasso ___"

DOWN

1. In Dante's "Inferno," each of these contains the soul of a sinner
2. Substitute for silk
3. "Waiting for Lefty" dramatist Clifford
4. Professional life
5. An ___ effort
6. Nile beast
7. Traveling companion of the apostle Paul
8. Provide coverage for
9. Key living room furniture
10. Scylla's danger
11. The American Mercury's founding editor
12. What Wednesday's child is full of
13. "Romeo ___ Juliet"
21. Wheel center
22. 1921 play that introduced the concept of robots
26. "Mefistofele" composer Arrigo
27. Baseball pioneer Doubleday
29. Nocturnal flier
30. Itsy bit
31. Pickle
32. Cleopatra's undoing
33. "___ of thousands!"
34. Girl in "Calvin and Hobbes" comics
35. Tornadoes and hurricanes, e.g.
39. First-aid material, collectively
40. Metal-bearing mineral
41. One of two Bible bks.
42. Paddle
44. Watering hole
47. "Go team!"
48. 1994 Kevin Smith film
49. Most sick
50. Shocking swimmer?
54. Loses steam
55. Railroad measure
56. Seiko rival
58. Radiant glow
59. 1917 abdicator
60. Carter player on "ER"

1	2	3		4	5	6	7	8		9	10	11	12	13
14				15						16				
17				18						19				
20			21						22					
23							24					25	26	27
			28		29	30				31	32			
33	34	35			36					37				
38			39	40				41	42					
43						44						45		
46				47	48				49	50				
51				52					53		54	55	56	
		57	58	59				60	61					
62	63				64						65			
66					67						68			
69					70						71			

61. 62-Down scheduling app

62. Device that isn't PC?

63. Anne Moody's autobiography "Coming of ___ in Mississippi"

7

ACROSS

1. March, e.g.
6. Alternative to that
10. Possession that might be frozen
15. From the beginning, to Brutus
16. Ingredient shaved from a rind, perhaps
17. Christine of "Chicago Hope"
18. Retro dance music genre
19. Second word of a famous rule
20. Deep-six
21. LP meas.
23. Underground thing, often
25. Drug giant ___ Lilly
26. Certain jury representative
30. Historian Doris Kearns ___
33. Clueless
34. King who died at the Battle of Thermopylae
35. Cold war jet
36. Pedro's pad
38. Virgo preceder
39. Novel whose title is enacted four times in this puzzle, with "The"
45. "The Tell-Tale Heart" monogram
46. Gardener's brand
47. They might have the best room in the dorm: Abbr.
49. Demographic peers
53. Most in need of a rub
56. Do the do over
57. Word before system or branch
58. Wall Street abbr.
59. Bi- quadrupled
61. AARP member: Abbr.
62. Scatter
65. ___ Sutra
67. Precious object, perhaps
71. Split to unite?
72. They've split
73. Reacted to fireworks, say
74. Having just taken up
75. War game
76. Polluted clouds

DOWN

1. Boiling over
2. ___-Wan Kenobi
3. Refusals
4. People who make the news, literally
5. To-do
6. Shih ___ (ancient breed)
7. With 57-Down, author of 39-Across
8. Analogy phrase
9. Eye-poker of slapstick
10. Parodist Yankovic and others
11. ___ fly (baseball play)
12. Astute
13. List ender
14. Some offensive basketball scores
22. Explorer whose name is often shouted in pools
24. Hoses' houses
26. End of a giant's refrain
27. Taking care of business
28. Prego rival
29. Like Beethoven
31. "Currently serving" military status
32. Chanel contemporary
34. Bert who was Garland's costar in 1939
37. White word on a road sign
40. Col.'s command
41. Not one
42. Rebuke to Brutus
43. "... ___ saw Elba"
44. "Fuzzy Wuzzy ___ bear ..."
48. Mo. town?
49. Up
50. Washer setting
51. Funds might be in it
52. Bob who played the announcer in "Major League"
54. Japanese mercenaries
55. Real riot
57. See 7-Down
60. Sitcom with the character Louie De Palma
63. Emissions org.
64. Soaked

Ghost Story

DANIEL A. FINAN

7

66. "Don't ___"
68. One of the five W's
69. Neurosurgeon's recording
70. Mormons, initially

8

ACROSS

1. Hardly verbose
6. Snacks that may be crunchy or soft
11. Bonkers
15. Similar
16. Shoelace tip
17. "Woe is me!"
18. Dumas classic about a trapped and disguised critter, with "The"?
21. Hunk of marble
22. Puff of smoke
23. Field larks
24. Memorial words
26. In the can
27. Greene classic about an icky Cold War correspondent?
33. Take by force
34. White House position
35. Gulf War missle
38. ___-di-dah
39. Intimate alternatives to lecture classes
43. Misspell, e.g.
44. ___ on the wrist
46. Castle security system
47. Giant crowd
49. Shaw classic about the nature of larvae?
53. Tall and thin
54. Jerk's beverage
55. Sea monster near Charybdis
58. Egg cell
60. Insignificant amounts
64. Kafka classic, and a process undergone by 18-, 27-, and 49-Across
67. Itty-bitty bit
68. Banish
69. Constellation with Betelgeuse
70. Destroy
71. Put off
72. Nicholas and Alexander, e.g.

DOWN

1. Bar bills
2. 12th Jewish month
3. Latvia's capital
4. Winter vehicles similar to bicycles
5. Poetic dusk
6. Setting for Melville's "Omoo"
7. Quite a while
8. YouTube offering
9. "Jingle Bells" preposition
10. Stay the night, say
11. Makes moist
12. Jai ___
13. Go without food for a day, say
14. Disapproving sounds
19. Branch offshoot?
20. One of a nautical trio
25. Ifs and ands partner
26. Anti-art art movement
27. Nocturnal mouse hunters
28. Russian river
29. Grammy-winning Amy Winehouse song
30. Water nymph
31. They can point you in the right direction
32. Sour-tasting
36. Pakistani language
37. Undesirable bit
40. Wafted
41. Brother to many
42. Place to keep garden equipment
45. Big name in sleeper cars
48. Soapbox speakers
50. Dorothy's last name
51. Shylock, e.g.
52. Circumstance companion
55. Tend, as sauce
56. ___ En-lai
57. Hairy hoax
58. Fail to include
59. Prairie rodent
61. 1980s supergroup with "Heat of the Moment"
62. Fashionable Christian
63. IRS IDs
65. Paul Bunyan's tool of choice
66. Stolen, slangily

Gregor Samsa's Bookshelf

KRISTIAN HOUSE

9

ACROSS

1. Watched
5. Be itinerant
9. ___ de plume (pseudonyms)
13. ___ Nostra
14. Tone in some old photojournalism
15. Bygone Greek theaters
16. Book banned for "racist language," as well as the word "sweat"
19. Harem room
20. "Don't rub ___"
21. Whipped dessert
22. Atlas abbr.
24. Google Maps suggestion: Abbr.
26. Relatively cool sun
27. Most-banned children's book series, for "occultism"
30. Cases of tools
31. Org. for Flyers and Blackhawks
32. Pres. who created the FCC
35. "That goes double for me"
37. Off the path
39. The "P" in MPG
40. "The Governator"
44. Smidgen
45. Book once challenged because its author was "known to have had an anti-business attitude"
47. Old actress Pola
50. Beseech
51. Early nights, in sonnets
52. After many delays
54. Makes a getaway
56. Gambling initials
58. Book banned for its graphic depiction of teen life and bullying
61. Too fastidious
62. Proof of ownership
63. NYC cultural center
64. Unsupported
65. Unchallenging
66. Offensive, to some

DOWN

1. Lover of Narcissus
2. "I'd rather not be the one to choose"
3. Even when not running, you can climb it
4. U.S. territory that's now two states: Abbr.
5. New awakening, as of knowledge
6. Revealing kind of shoe
7. Make public
8. Stodgy schoolteacher
9. Without complication
10. Allen Ginsberg, e.g.
11. Well-read group
12. More with it
14. Word after "ready"
17. Historian banned by Caligula
18. Backwoods folk
23. At one time, at one time
25. End of a direction?
27. Don't bother reading
28. Brouhaha
29. "If ___ Hammer"
32. Henceforth
33. What mailed parcels are marked with
34. Private played by Matt Damon
36. Clumsy
38. Thing it's hard to swim against
41. Point
42. Leopard-like cats
43. According to the rules
45. Delphi prophet
46. Make a home, so to speak
47. Birth-related
48. Prefix with centrism
49. Read between the lines
53. Handheld book bag
55. West jailed for obscenity after the debut of her first Broadway play
57. Bric-a-___
59. Org. with lots of secrets
60. Australian runner

Unreadable

T CAMPBELL

10

ACROSS

1. Scandinavian language from which "tundra" comes
5. Wonka factory casualty Augustus
10. Drill
14. "The Sopranos" actor Robert
15. Window alternative, on a plane
16. Fast-growing city near Provo
17. ___-war (predatory bird)
18. Remote target?
19. Some backyard gatherings, for short
20. Novelist Charlotte's Jurassic predecessor?
23. Prenatal test, for short
24. Deceive
28. Cappuccino topper
32. "___ and Sensibility"
33. ___ Vegas
36. Storyteller Roald's primitive relation?
39. Adolph of publishing
41. Like notebook paper
42. "The dele's off"?
43. Playwright David's prehistoric cousin?
46. U.S.N.A. grad
47. Half of a Muppet duo
48. Exodus peak
50. Caught, as with a tree branch
53. Inhaled tobacco
57. Epic poet's Pleistocene progenitor?
61. Abandon, as a lover
64. DC-9, e.g.
65. Peck's partner
66. Matinee or teen follower
67. Spasm
68. Descartes' therefore
69. Like many modern cars, shapewise
70. On-ramp sign
71. Salon sound

DOWN

1. Lion, in Swahili
2. Something to keep you from your dreams?
3. Exciting baseball scenario
4. Disaffected, in a way
5. Scandal suffix
6. Ullmann and Tyler
7. Bones: Lat.
8. Chemical used in some explosives
9. Big name in biology lab dishes
10. Winter Olympics conveyances
11. Planet, poetically
12. Not an elective: Abbr.
13. Ambulance letters
21. Of two minds
22. KGB state
25. Related maternally
26. Quite white
27. Back muscles, to lifters
29. Hard to get a hold of
30. Cripple
31. Kournikova and Quindlen
33. Home Depot rival
34. Oak-to-be
35. Some ethnic Zimbabweans
37. She went from Bruce to Ashton
38. Tree of knowledge garden
40. Just a hair
44. Kid's interlocking block
45. Stun with a gun
49. Yard divisions
51. Like some nests
52. Deepak Chopra's birthplace
54. Road reversal
55. Toadstools and truffles, e.g.
56. SLR setting
58. Like hen's teeth
59. Hydroxyl compound
60. Bassoonist's need
61. Forward sail
62. Rite answer?
63. Everything bagel topper

Literary Ancestors

BRENT SVERDLOFF

10

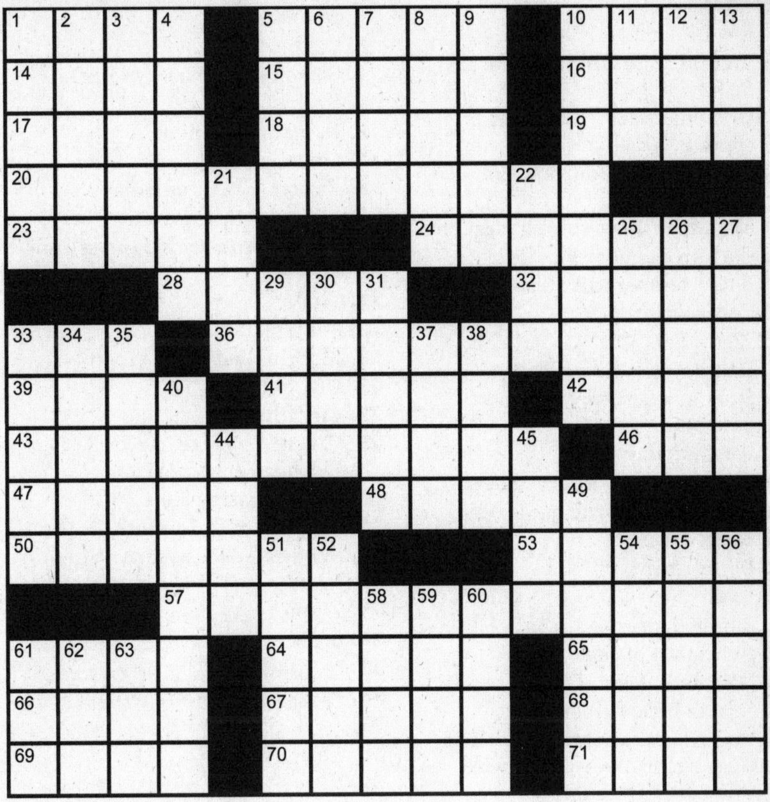

11

ACROSS

1. Vienna State Opera conductor Seiji
6. "A Momentary ___ of Reason" (Pink Floyd album)
11. New Orleans' Bourbon and others: Abbr.
14. Magazine cover subject, casually
15. Certain calendar starter
16. Water temperature tester
17. Controls
18. "Peter Pan" girl
19. Rainbow shape
20. Start of a quote by James Baldwin
23. Persia, today
24. Shorebird with a curved beak
25. Second part of the quote
32. Sacks
33. Deportment
34. "Bali ___"
37. Bumped into
38. Third part of the quote
41. NYC line, once
42. Santa's little helper
43. "A man may see how this world/ Goes with no eyes. Look with thine ears" speaker
44. Little biter
45. Fourth part of the quote
50. Abandon one's dreams?
52. Unlikely to leave things out
53. End of the quote
59. Forensic drama series
60. Ways to a person's heart?
61. Symbol of slowness
64. Sweetie
65. Sister of Melpomene
66. Handy
67. Heart chart: Abbr.
68. Didn't stop
69. Guided a raft

DOWN

1. Suffix with hill or bull
2. "___ and the Art of Motorcycle Maintenance"
3. Bajillions
4. Search engine query return
5. Soak up
6. Bargain-basement
7. Once again
8. Phnom ___, Cambodia
9. Masochistic beginning?
10. Nestlé Drumstick Sundae Cone maker
11. Linger
12. Tokyo gateway
13. Marginal religious groups
21. Util. bill enc.
22. Tire filler
25. "Then We ___ to the End" (Joshua Ferris novel)
26. Figure skating turn
27. Job that pulls in a lot?
28. Syndicated horoscope writer Sydney
29. Zippo
30. Sushi selection
31. "___ luck?"
35. Al Jazeera viewer, perhaps
36. ___-bitty
38. Final: Abbr.
39. Visit
40. Former Mideast initials
44. Become a fan of
46. Originally
47. Something to sing in
48. Write
49. Prepares to go after a fly?
50. Manufacturer of the drugs Valium and Avastin
51. Reassuring words
54. Winnebago owner, e.g.
55. Blood fluids
56. "Gorillas in the Mist" author Fossey
57. Not had by
58. Follow closely
62. Land in la mer
63. Fronted

Taking the Reins

BRENDAN EMMETT QUIGLEY

12

ACROSS

1. President after JFK
4. Pitcher's stat
7. Car's set
13. Tennessee's state flower
15. Citrusy beverage once enjoyed by the tsars
17. Sweater-eating bug
18. Nathaniel Philbrick book about the expedition that named Antarctica
19. Power failure
21. 1051, on a monument
22. Officeholders
23. Goat's opposite
24. Michelle who graduated from the same high school as Barack Obama
25. 5th-century AD pope known as "the Great"
27. 5th-century BC Persian emperor known as "the Great"
29. Potato-preparing implements
31. Christopher Cokinos book about meteorites that follow explorers and scientists as far as Antarctica
33. Down in the dumps
34. Tom Clancy thriller set in Antarctica
35. Stunt biker's bike
38. Franklin W. Dixon mystery that sends the Hardy Boys to Antarctica
40. "Got that?"
43. "Our Gang" members
44. Astronauts Bean and Shepard
45. Even alternative
47. Neuter, as a horse
48. Where 24-Down is the resident puzzlemaster
49. Mexican Mrs.
50. "Scram!"
52. Kelly Tyler-Lewis book about a party of explorers stranded in Antarctica
56. "___ Fishin'"
57. Kenny Loggins hit on the "Top Gun" soundtrack
58. Many an MIT grad: Abbr.
59. Very hot, blue celestial bodies
60. Egg ___ (yuletide quaff)
61. Nine-digit ID

DOWN

1. Ride to the prom, perhaps
2. Hubbub
3. Had the shakes
4. Celtic language that gave us "hubbub"
5. Regret
6. "Likewise"
7. Modern hotel amenity, for computer users
8. Old bat
9. Photo blowup: Abbr.
10. Star, in Strasbourg
11. "My Fair Lady" lyricist
12. Final authorities
14. Dr. Zhivago portrayer Omar
16. Serious promise
20. Paints used in Matisse's "Blue Nudes"
24. Crossword-editing subject of the documentary "Wordplay"
25. Kmart's founder
26. Bible possessive
27. The shakes
28. Gin fruits
30. Yoga posture
32. Summertime setting in Washington, D.C.
35. Bookstores acquired by Barnes & Noble (and liquidated in January 2010)
36. Baseboard strips
37. Some big T-shirts
38. Hamilton's bill
39. Historic cold spell
40. Is incapable of
41. Top dogs
42. Mom or dad
46. Jason Bourne portrayer Matt
49. CCCP divisions
50. Rare blood type, briefly

Cold Reading

BYRON WALDEN

51. Coastal bird
53. JFK alternative, in NYC
54. "___ the land of the free . . ."
55. Rock musician Brian

13

ACROSS

1. neeuq a semoceb ohw lrig elttiL
6. Lhasa ___
10. One-eyed signal
14. Copies, with a VCR
15. Faucet problem
16. Plant in many a lotion
17. Fantasy garment that may grant invisibility
18. Sup (on)
19. One may be drawn in the sand to make a point
20. elzzup siht ni seulc drawkcab eht daer ot deen uoy tahW
23. Cunning
26. Mentally stable
27. Half of a Worcestershire sauce duo
28. Actor Corey of "Lucas"
31. "That's IT!"
35. Torah pointer
36. kcans-rekcins seog edalb laprov a erehw meoP
38. Canal across New York State
40. Gabor or Perón
41. Olden times
42. raey a eseht fo 463 evah eW
47. Business abbr.
48. Sawbuck
49. Financial sci.
50. Take a breather
51. Gold or silver sources
53. Where trains stop: Abbr.
55. emeht s'elzzup siht rof noitaripsnI
60. ___ cloud (whence comets)
61. Mild rebukes
62. "Jack Sprat could ___ fat"
66. Crispy Mexican food
67. Channel for checking scores
68. Song line
69. Eliot Ness, e.g.
70. Congresswoman's area, briefly
71. snwap dna sgnik htiw deyalp emaG

DOWN

1. ". . . yadda, yadda, yadda"
2. Silent ___ (presidential nickname)
3. First sale of a stock
4. Renter's agreement
5. Demands a reason
6. Extra, for short
7. Puritan
8. Croons
9. Like some flea markets
10. Passed on the sidewalk, say
11. Hip bone prefix
12. Kid's taboo
13. Boat stabilizer
21. Aleutian island
22. "I've Got the Music ___"
23. Most crafty
24. When repeated, a herald's call
25. Angle measure
29. Cake decorator
30. Silver screen show
32. Double reed user
33. Home to Aslan
34. Casts out
37. Legendary former NYC Top 40 radio station
39. Ralph Kramden's pal
43. Frau's guy
44. Picked up the tab
45. Neighbor of Swed.
46. Lets a line loose
52. Palermo pardon
54. Kills, as a dragon
55. Former Senator Trent
56. Great growing dirt
57. Largest of the dolphin family
58. Motor oil additives
59. Ain't proper?
63. Uno, due, ___
64. Medical research arm of the Dept. of Human Services
65. Infrequent: Abbr.

dnalrednoW tsaP elzzuP

RYAN GENOVESE

14

ACROSS

1. 43,560 square feet
5. Pause on the runway
9. Slogan-creating guy, perhaps
14. False front
15. Norway's patron saint
16. River that flows around Notre Dame
17. Pull up a chair next to
19. Rudolph's master
20. Horror author Clive at a sideshow?
22. Group of eight
23. Threader's target
24. Lebanon neighbor
27. Blunder
31. Horror author Bram working in a mine?
35. Move along the runway
36. Mai Tai liquor
37. Completely consumed
39. Give a bad review to
40. Acutely eager
42. Timely horror author Anne?
44. Pre-2002 Spanish coins
46. Leases
47. "On the Road" narrator Paradise
48. "The Plague" writer Albert
51. Cowardly, like horror author Stephen?
57. It was dry in the song "American Pie"
58. Resolved
60. "___ you clever!"
61. Paleontologist's prize
62. Servers with spigots
63. Basil-based pasta sauce
64. Iditarod vehicle
65. Comfort

DOWN

1. Buffoon
2. In vogue
3. Pro ___ (in proportion)
4. Involve in trouble
5. Claim as fact
6. ___ Oyl (Swee'Pea's babysitter, often)
7. Former Egyptian president Anwar
8. Daredevil Robbie's dad
9. Appraises pitchblende, say
10. Most beloved
11. Weasel cousin
12. Part of A.M.
13. Within a stone's throw
18. Containerize
21. Lebanese University city
24. Send to the junkyard
25. "___ gotta be kidding me!"
26. Harold of "Ghostbusters"
27. Aid in choosing sides?
28. Hard-to-miss putt
29. To the letter
30. Cone-dropping trees
32. Dish cooked in cornhusks
33. Big name in elevators
34. Kesey who wrote "One Flew Over the Cuckoo's Nest"
38. 18th-century wig
41. Mountaineer's trip down
43. Chimney soot, e.g.
45. Grow fond of
48. December song
49. Unescorted
50. Like Black Beauty or Flicka
51. Join in an ovation
52. "Come to me, Rover!"
53. Burl of ballads
54. Pen points
55. Screenwriter Ephron
56. Paintball weapons
59. Mao ___-Tung

Fright Club

PATRICK JORDAN

15

ACROSS

1. On the apex
5. Honolulu veranda
10. Dissertation writers' degs.
14. Solidarity leader Walesa
15. Full speed ahead
16. "On the Waterfront" director Kazan
17. Typographically-eccentric poet
19. Defunct science magazine
20. Harper Valley org.
21. Shakespearean villain
22. How spam goes, usually
24. Saki's real name
26. "The results ___" (election-night announcement)
27. "High ___" (Maxwell Anderson play)
28. Is a ham
31. Common dog moniker
34. Puppeteer Bil or Cora
35. Popular campground initials
36. Elliot of the Mamas & the Papas
37. Jabs
38. Long-lasting hairdo
39. Pikes Peak, e.g.: Abbr.
40. Seven-time A.L. batting champ Rod
41. "For Whom the Bell Tolls" poet
42. Incorporated gradually
44. "You've got mail" co.
45. Ubiquitous MP3 players
46. "The Time Machine" author
50. UTEP locale
52. D. H. Lawrence ranch city
53. Want-ad letters
54. Sound from Simba
55. Creator of Horatio Hornblower
58. Superabundance
59. Cute eucalyptus eater
60. Fairy-tale meanie
61. Stewpot, or its contents
62. Cobbler's supplies
63. Meeting caller, perhaps

DOWN

1. First Hebrew letter
2. They're enameled
3. William of ___ (philosopher known for his razor)
4. Dien Bien ___, Vietnam
5. Hedy of Hollywood
6. Pancho, to Cisco
7. Prefix with second
8. Company in a 2009 employee bonus controversy
9. Peace of mind providers, perhaps
10. Headquarters of Caterpillar
11. Author called the "Sage of Baltimore"
12. Lindsay Lohan's mother
13. Verbalized
18. Not of legal age
23. Socially inept sort
25. Four Corners natives
26. "___ from the Bridge" (Arthur Miller play)
28. Like some old buckets
29. Severed, as paper
30. Unchanged
31. Dudley Do-Right's org.
32. Swearword
33. Nobel Prize winner for literature in 2001
34. Natasha's cartoon sidekick
37. Areas for racehorses
38. Flag's place
40. Boardroom VIPs
41. Use a divining rod
43. Athens rival
44. Athenian marketplaces
46. Non-Polynesian Hawaiian
47. "Gimme that!"
48. Suggestive glances
49. Painful skin spots
50. "Cogito, ___ sum"
51. Lounge around
52. Big name in nonstick cookware
56. ___ Locks (Sault Ste. Marie canals)
57. Cry and cry

Men of Letters

DENNY BAKER

16

ACROSS

1. *"Odyssey" poet
6. Travel book features
10. Dollars and cents
14. Love, to Dario Fo
15. "___, Sing America" (Langston Hughes poem)
16. Killer whale
17. *"Paradise Regained" author
19. Unaccounted-for soldiers
20. "No way, ___!"
21. Sci-fi author Gaiman
22. Chinua Achebe's "Things Fall ___"
23. Use an online engine
25. "A Man in Full" author Tom
26. Word form for "middle"
29. Byproducts of sesame and olives, e.g.
31. Mysterious sight in the sky
32. He flew too close to the sun
36. Facility
40. *"The Garden of Forking Paths" author
43. Yes ___ question
44. Climb
45. No longer working: Abbr.
46. Word of warning
48. "If ___ Million Dollars"
50. "Cry, the Beloved Country" novelist
53. Spiral-shaped pasta
57. Upper-crust
58. "You can say that again!"
59. Gentle animal
63. "Bull Durham" actor Robbins
64. *"Light in My Darkness" autobiographer
67. "Foucault's Pendulum" novelist Umberto
68. Late humorist Molly
69. Contradict
70. Money in Matsuyama
71. Make fun of

72. Like the four authors in this puzzle's starred clues

DOWN

1. Muslim pilgrimage
2. Melville book subtitled "A Narrative of Adventures in the South Seas"
3. Scale of mineral hardness
4. "A Lesson Before Dying" novelist ___ J. Gaines
5. Georgia rock band since 1980
6. Middle-distance runner
7. Web site?
8. Cabana
9. Hamlet, to Gertrude
10. Beethoven, e.g.
11. Popular font
12. Neck warmer
13. Rapidity
18. Bill Bryson's "___ Sunburned Country"
22. Tool that makes holes
24. Cleveland's lake
26. Stephen King canine
27. ___ effort
28. Norse goddess of fate
30. Book ID
33. Highland family
34. Subject of 18-down
35. Wrestler Flair
37. The Taj Mahal's town
38. Tree-to-be
39. Spanish 101 verb
41. Unseen character in a Samuel Beckett play
42. Mythological chief god
47. ___ wonder (musician who never repeats initial success)
49. Jewish school group
50. "The Little Rascals" dog
51. Writer Munro or McDermott
52. Shakespeare's title Athenian
54. Signs of the future
55. Future perfect, e.g.
56. Tattoo artist's supply
60. "___ said was . . ."
61. Lo ___ noodles

Visionaries

MATT GAFFNEY

16

62. Raised
65. Genesis palindrome
66. Flow's counterpart

17

ACROSS

1. Golf tournament often featuring celebrities
6. Scholarly volume
10. Lacking, along the Loire
14. River mouth near New Orleans, e.g.
15. Wild long-horned goat
16. Samoa's capital
17. Periodically updated websites about the Constitution?
20. '60s radical gp.
21. Saturn SUV
22. Angels on high
23. Play the ponies, say
24. Actress Vardalos
25. Hacked missive?
33. Olympic skater Harding
34. Comfy shoes
35. Season starter?
36. Tour of duty
37. "Scent ___ Woman"
38. Inuit wear
40. Weed
41. Juilliard degs.
42. Wickerwork wood
43. VoIP contact from the forest?
47. Prince Valiant's son
48. "Big" British clock
49. Pretty prestigious rating, in the Michelin Guide
53. Prohibit
54. "___ Lay Dying"
57. Messages between Kent college students about where 2 meet up ltr?
60. Pelt
61. French film
62. Absolutely perfect
63. Baja bravos
64. Early Chinese dynasty
65. Cakewalk course

DOWN

1. Adobe files: Abbr.
2. Bassoonist's purchase
3. Former GM division, casually
4. Finished off a hero?
5. Admire with astonishment
6. Piece that may have a 10-point Q
7. Japanese sash
8. Pigsty
9. Goes longer
10. Muslim's deferential bow
11. Each
12. On the horizon
13. Give lip to
18. Not manual
19. Spreadable cheese
23. ___ Mawr College
25. "The Chosen" author Chaim
26. Togetherness
27. "Gotta run!"
28. Words on some diet foods
29. Online dough
30. Mathematics Awareness Month
31. Ticked off
32. Cordelia's dad
33. 768 make a gal.
38. Businessman's symbol of authority
39. Z-zebra link
41. Butterfly known for its migration pattern
44. Attaches, after cutting
45. One-named Harper's Bazaar illustrator
46. Cyberauction site
49. Cuatro y cuatro
50. Bed part?
51. "The Neverending Story" author
52. Part of baseball's Triple Crown
53. La ___, Los Angeles
54. Guitars, so to speak
55. Command to Rex
56. Cuba, por ejemplo
58. Sushi bar sea urchin
59. Writer LeShan

The Times They Are a-Changin'

KRISTIAN HOUSE

18

ACROSS

1. Jacob Marley or Hamlet's father, e.g.
6. Float on the breeze
10. Stupefy
14. City near Boys Town, Nebraska
15. Declare openly
16. De-coupled couples
17. Compound that keeps away cockroaches
18. Title fit for a king
19. Bro and sis
20. "Roger & Me" documentarian
23. Deg. for a corp. type
26. Coral island
27. "Jake and the ___" (CBS series)
28. Ski lodge quaffs
30. Outset, colloquially
32. Portrayer of "Bluto" Blutarsky and "Joliet" Jake
34. Frequent tattoo honoree
37. Bills with pyramids
38. Domino dot
39. Use a squeegee, say
40. "Little Red Riding Hood" prop
41. Daughter of fast-food magnate Dave
45. "Silly" birds
46. Nature trail devotees
47. Conch's shape
50. "Casino Royale" author Fleming
51. "Charlotte's Web" setting
52. Group whose names appear, respectively, at the beginning of 20-, 32-, and 41-Across
56. Subject matter
57. Pizzeria device
58. Fifty-fifty
62. Lessens the intensity of
63. Pamplona runner, to the locals
64. "Fab Four" nickname
65. " . . . or ___!"
66. "Time of Hope" author C. P.___
67. Condescending one

DOWN

1. Will Arnett character on "Arrested Development"
2. M.D. employer, perhaps
3. Handheld wake maker
4. Bogus
5. Travis Bickle's vehicle
6. Wishy-___ (ineffectual)
7. Reebok rival
8. Cry on a course
9. Shakespeare's "___ Night"
10. Explorer Hernando
11. Self-evident truth
12. Lion's dinner
13. German steelworks center
21. Study, before burgling
22. Trio in an O. Henry title
23. Menial occupation, so to speak
24. Daniel whose rifle was "Tick Licker"
25. Pulsed with pain
29. Iron-___ (heat-applied decals)
30. Mentor
31. Set eyes on
33. Certain hosp. staffers
34. Wordless performers
35. Illusory illustrations
36. Like many a teenager's room
39. Convex-bottomed pan
41. Have an erosive effect
42. Conger traps
43. Malaysian's neighbor to the north
44. Holds back
45. 1978 vehicle for John Travolta
47. Hammett hero Sam
48. Mortal danger
49. Agenda entries
50. "You don't have to tell me that"
53. Stratford-upon-___
54. Aptly named CD "burning" software
55. Small surface measure, for short
59. Game with 108 cards
60. Into the past
61. Grouped offering, on eBay

Darling Threesome

PATRICK JORDAN

ACROSS

1. Rock star's gear
4. Barter
8. Responses to doctor's orders?
11. Shock
15. Conk out
16. Alternative to elite, on a keyboard
17. Lady killer
19. Places to score 88-Across
21. Ajax, for one
22. Its working title was "A Jewish Patient Begins His Analysis"
24. Number after deux
25. Gun, slangily
26. Born, in France
27. Its working title was "Strangers from Within"
34. Exclusive group
37. Tribe once part of the Winnebago
38. Springfield shopkeeper Nahasapeemapetilon
39. Its working title was "Something That Happened"
46. Gets on one's soapbox
49. Boxer who first defeated Foreman
50. Site of Mobutu Sese Seko's kleptocracy
51. Its working title was "He Do the Police in Different Voices"
56. Sydney's state: Abbr.
57. ___ fixe (persistent thought)
58. American Indians who sometimes lived in wickiups
61. Its working title was "Trimalchio in West Egg"
67. Hither partner
68. Strange-seeming
69. Like some beers
73. Its working title was "First Impressions"
80. Something to keep you from reaching your dreams?
81. Wilde, Carroll, and Tolkien, as students
82. Exam administered alone
83. Musical gym accessory
84. Trapeze artist's fallback
85. Bacon cheeseburgers, to a Hasid
86. Star golfer Michelle
87. Units of weight for elephants
88. They're scored in 19-Across: Abbr.

DOWN

1. Highly skilled
2. Person under eighteen
3. Three-time Cy Young Award winner Martinez
4. A letter or number, on "Sesame Street"
5. Skid row sort
6. ___-deucey (backgammon variant)
7. You might not get to do it before going to jail
8. Creator of the March sisters
9. Actor Ian who played Puck
10. Stair
11. Former Wimbledon champ Novotná
12. Italian family that included three popes
13. Many a homeowner in America
14. Rich Eastern European cakes
18. "2001" computer
20. Valuable Scrabble piece
23. "I'd like a nonfat half-___ latte with soy milk"
28. 2016 Summer Olympics host, casually
29. Rapper and actor Mos ___
30. Shed tool
31. Pilot's landing guess: Abbr.
32. "Happy Days" character who literally jumped the shark, with "the"
33. Helen of Troy's mother
34. You shouldn't put one in front of a horse, it's said
35. Brightly colored fish
36. Ditty
40. Quotable actress West
41. Like Tiny Tim
42. OSS successor
43. Ho Chi ___

First Names

MATT MATERA

44. Gaelic language
45. Tidings
47. Kindling component
48. ___ City (Baghdad neighborhood)
52. "Understand?"
53. Green or peppermint, e.g.
54. Turner who led a slave insurrection
55. Inning enders, often
59. Is everywhere
60. '80s star Lauper
61. One who may have a high words-per-minute rate
62. He congratulated himself for finding a plum

63. Exile to Elba or St. Helena, e.g.
64. As of yet
65. Important econ. indicator
66. Crackerjack
70. Cuban pitcher Luis
71. Going through an embarrassing outbreak, as a teenager
72. Cockroaches, e.g.
74. Remove, as a hat
75. CPR pro
76. Once again
77. Not yet final, in law
78. Trade show
79. "Benny and ___" (1993 Johnny Depp romcom)

20

ACROSS

1. 2006 Pixar film
5. Magic power
9. Steinbeck's "The Grapes of ___"
14. Gait in a harness race
15. Mars's Greek counterpart
16. Vietnam's capital
17. Fictional resident of Manderley
20. Sideways football toss
21. Bear witness (to)
22. Young fellow
23. Eyes provocatively
25. Fictional resident of Glamis Castle
29. Pen name for Dickens
32. Took too much, briefly
33. Ott and Brooks
34. High-heeled Astaire
36. Loser to Ike
38. Illuminated
39. Some short-necked ducks
40. City in Michael Moore's "Roger & Me"
41. "Oh, ___ it now"
43. Touched down
44. Sargasso, e.g.
45. Fictional resident of Green Gables
48. Pasted
49. Driver's docs., e.g.
50. Toast from Tevye
53. Deutsche marks?
57. Fictional resident of Longbourn
60. "Funeral Blues" poet
61. Stringed instrument
62. Pitchfork prong
63. Sedge warblers' habitat
64. "Days of Grace" memoirist Arthur
65. Envelope abbr.

DOWN

1. Key below "Shift" on many keyboards
2. Vicinity
3. Gen. ___ E. Lee
4. "Aja" band
5. Paving material
6. Word before exam or hygiene
7. "The Beverly Hillbillies" patriarch
8. Verb ending?
9. Clichéd headgear for the good guy
10. Carries on
11. Feed the pot for poker
12. An alert person may be on hers
13. "Sugar Lips" trumpeter Al
18. Hastily prepare for midterms
19. Whitman or Disney
23. Normatively required, perhaps
24. Exploits
25. Goldbricks
26. Confuse
27. Noted British chef Smith
28. Canadian songstress Dion
29. Beginning and end
30. Basic skateboarding trick
31. Piquant
35. Start of many pre-Christmas letters
37. Neapolitans, e.g.
42. Thumb cover
46. Desensitize
47. Wasting time, perhaps
48. Looked steadily, as into a crystal ball
50. King in a Shakespearean tragedy
51. Helpful discovery for Holmes
52. Cover up
53. "This could be a problem!"
54. ICU part
55. Big top
56. Tommy gun
58. 1996 role for Madonna
59. Sequel to "Angela's Ashes"

There's No Place Like Home

DONNA LEVIN

21

ACROSS

1. "The Tin Drum" author Gunter
6. The Union Jack, e.g.
10. Rip to shreds
14. Heart attachment
15. Puerto ___
16. "SportsCenter" network
17. Dog treats
18. Prefix meaning "within"
19. Indy 500 units
20. "Ulysses" character whose name refers to the Greek architect of the Labyrinth
23. Like some nouns: Abbr.
24. Support piece?
25. "Trial of the Century" figure Kaelin
28. He's represented by a narrow-minded "Ulysses" character referred to as "The Citizen"
34. One of the Trasks from "East of Eden"
35. Wade opponent
36. Poi party
37. Curvy brass instrument
38. Stockpile
40. Magazine on the rack near "Money"
41. 1960s space chimp
43. Mr. ___ (baseball mascot)
44. Slightly open
45. She represents Penelope in "Ulysses"
49. Word after maiden or pen
50. Hemingway collection "In ___ Time"
51. "___, It's Cold Outside"
53. Race of island dwellers in "The Odyssey" who lend their name to a "Ulysses" episode
60. Alexander who claimed he was "in charge" after Reagan was shot
61. With all one's marbles
62. Kevin who played a TV Hercules
63. DVIII doubled
64. Novelist Murdoch
65. Author played by Hal Holbrook
66. Appearance
67. Rentable pads: Abbr.
68. On pins and needles

DOWN

1. Tells a secret
2. Tooth part
3. "Rule, Britannia" composer Thomas
4. Parent from a later marriage, perhaps
5. Malia's sister
6. "J'accuse" language
7. Soprano Jenny, the "Swedish Nightingale"
8. Part of a Molière play
9. They're sometimes tough to say
10. Like scandalous biographies
11. Jacob's biblical twin
12. iPad programs, for short
13. ER workers
21. Guinness Book suffix
22. Storyline shape
25. Last name in Top 40 radio
26. "A Bell for ___" (John Hersey novel)
27. Cancer inhibitor derived from yew tree bark
29. Muse of love poetry
30. Romaine, alternately
31. Occult board name
32. Airline in "Catch Me If You Can"
33. City paired with La Paz, Bolivia
38. Food of the gods
39. "Blazing Saddles" director Brooks
42. Liquor used to make some fizz drinks
44. Generic location in print ads to show how an address looks
46. Bald-headed Brynner
47. Really worry (over)
48. Sallie ___ (student loan company)
52. "That's enough!" in Italian
53. Yell at the curbside
54. Home with honey
55. Baseball field coverer

Homer Loans

MATT JONES

21

56. Page or ream, e.g
57. Part of QED
58. Hank Aaron has the most of them all-time
59. "Jeopardy!" studio
60. "I wonder . . ."

22

ACROSS

1. Underway
6. Sam with 82 PGA Tour event wins
11. Lobster restaurant handout
14. Town north of Bangor
15. Bird on the Great Seal of the United States
16. Nabokov heroine
17. "Getting all sentimental, Virginia?"?
19. Corn eater's throwaway
20. Paint layer
21. Suffix for real or romantic
22. Like the original installments of "Great Expectations"
24. Not the real thing
26. Polar bear's perch
28. Drainage reservoir
30. Draw in
33. Garden plot
36. Wood-eating beetle, for one
38. Covered in goo
39. Yankee slugger, to fans and headline writers
41. Opera legend Beverly
43. Cut, as a tuft
44. Like winter coats
46. Upside-down tree hanger
48. Outer: Prefix
49. Doggie day-care providers
51. File folder features
53. Some college assignments
55. Light in the refrigerator?
59. Reached the finish line
61. Alias signaler
63. Sheltered at sea
64. Word before "blast off!"
65. "C'mon, Karl, everybody's doing it!"
68. School booster gp.
69. Aspirin or ibuprofen, briefly
70. Footnote abbr. for a work already mentioned
71. Slithery swimmer
72. Ticket remains
73. Young'uns

DOWN

1. Lawn bowling game
2. Slipup
3. Spanish paintings such as "The Disasters of War"
4. Namath's 1969 Super Bowl foil
5. Contrary start
6. Starts a suit, maybe
7. Wynonna's mom
8. One of a Freudian trio
9. Totally wrong
10. Flaws
11. "Not so close, Thomas"
12. Object of a Fox hunt that millions of Americans follow avidly?
13. Darling
18. Thingamajigs
23. Husbands of countesses
25. Where you might get a soaking
27. Dealer's domain
29. Prudish
31. 909, to the Romans
32. What a cpoy editor is supposed to find
33. Pitcher's no-no
34. Tribe that named a lake
35. "John, hand out the cards already!"
37. Building extension
40. Thick-skulled
42. German POW camp
45. Draws up a blueprint for
47. "Sex and the City" channel
50. Most recent
52. "Beetle Bailey" camp
54. Respectful title in "A Passage to India"
56. Soul singer Roberta
57. Raptor's retreat
58. Scholarly works
59. Sulk
60. Poker pot builder
62. Virtually all the "Lord of the Flies" characters
66. Sigma follower
67. Trendy

Addressing the Author

LYNN LEMPEL

23

ACROSS

1. Dance unit
5. Ewe cry
8. Wax on a love letter, e.g.
13. Volcano flower?
14. Flirtatious head move
15. Circle about
16. Chinese animals celebrated in 1997 and 2009
17. Penguin Classic set in New England
19. Venting session
21. Wagered sum
22. Declare with purpose
23. "The Luncheon on the Grass" painter
26. Much-anticipated elementary school time
28. Penguin Classic set in Russia
32. What kept Hans Andersen's princess awake
33. Correspond in case or person
34. Short ribs measurement
38. Home to Asmara
40. File away
43. "The Better Man for a Better America" candidate
44. Spud
46. Gun on the street?
47. Penguin Classic set in France
51. Hardest part of hitting for the cycle, often
54. Inclined
55. Fabled layer of golden eggs
56. "Richard III" portrayer McKellen
58. ___ bar
62. Penguin Classic set in Germany
66. Thing next to a barn, often
67. "The Future of Atomic Energy" author Enrico
68. Ernst & Young workers, for short
69. Squeaked by, with "out"
70. Catches, as a varmint

DOWN

1. Opening
2. Urban conveyance
3. "The coldest winter I ___ spent was a summer in San Francisco" (Twain)
4. Canal locale
5. "R.U.R." laborer, slangily
6. Leaving after the barbecue?
7. Quickly, quickly
8. Relax, as one's tone
9. Stray from the straight and narrow
10. Of too fine a character for
11. Rides to special events
12. Goulash and gumbo
14. Like many early adopters of new technologies
18. Sushi seaweed
20. Capital of Senegal
24. Inserted list of corrections
25. Pro shop object
27. June Carter's husband
28. Ripped off
29. One of "The Twelve Caesars"
30. Hit, as with a fine
31. Felix, relative to Oscar
35. Old Italian bread?
36. Allege as fact
37. Crowd of quail
39. Short-term worker, perhaps
41. Shuts down, then starts up
42. Friend with benefits?
45. Something for a roadie to carry
48. Excuses, excuses
49. Darlin'
50. The Bounty or the Nautilus, e.g.
51. Petty crime, perhaps
52. Send to another lawyer, say
53. Prefix with red
57. Mild compliment
59. ___ torch
60. K-6 sch.
61. Got on one's mount

International Affairs

ANNE BRETHAUER

63. Little brat
64. Energy Star org.
65. Posed for a portrait

ACROSS

1. "The ___ of John and Yoko"
7. Reverent address
11. Suffix for video rigs attached to helmets, etc.
14. Andre who took many opens
15. Northern European capital
16. Ab ___ (from the start)
17. Declaration in the first line of a T. S. Eliot poem
19. Away's partner
20. '50s White House initials
21. Chapeau filler
22. Shaving lotion brand
23. Where 35-Across should have scuttled "across the floors," had he "been a pair of ragged claws"
27. Winter apples
32. Mario and Luigi, at times
33. He made his living in fur
34. Wish granters of myth
35. Title character of a T. S. Eliot poem in "The Waste Land and Other Poems"
41. Opera about an opera singer
42. Old-time actress Palmer
43. Northerly wind common in southern France
46. Made corrections to
48. What it is for 35-Across "to say just what I mean"
50. Per, slangily
51. Dancing girl in "Return of the Jedi"
53. Dallas sch. where the Mustangs play: Abbr.
56. ___ Paulo, Brazil
57. What, in the last line, might "wake us" before "we drown"
61. Hour div.
62. Manages, with "out"
63. Hereditary
64. "___ Poetica"
65. "The Devil ___ Down to Georgia"
66. Honey source

DOWN

1. Like some hair transplant candidates
2. Got on in years
3. Tardy
4. Baton Rouge campus, for short
5. Entry-level position, often: Abbr.
6. Process food?
7. "Psycho" setting
8. Andiron residue
9. Ginger ___
10. Common Jamaican address
11. With 45-Down, what 35-Across "measured out my life with"
12. 2010 James Cameron blockbuster
13. Soggy ground
18. Elisha's last name and Redding's first
22. Ache treater's drug
24. Water holder
25. Half an Orkan farewell
26. It hardly matters
27. Old Indian dominion
28. Member of NATO
29. Mo. town
30. Convertible cover option
31. Bobbling a grounder and dropping a fly, e.g.
34. 4.0, perhaps
36. Those, in La Mancha
37. 651, to Caesar
38. Played out, like a joke
39. The Browns, on the scoreboard
40. Tease
43. Noxious vapors
44. Damage
45. See 11-Down
46. Tar Heel State university
47. Van Peebles who wrote and starred in "Sweet Sweetback's Baadasssss Song"
49. Toot one's own horn
52. Tip-top rating
53. "Shoo!"
54. Introduction to physics?
55. Software buyer
57. Chop down

What a Love Song

VIC FLEMING AND BONNIE GENTRY

58. Island musical accompaniment
59. John Gray's "Martians"
60. Business letters

25

ACROSS

1. Sec'y, e.g.
5. Coop birds
9. Sending a duplicate, for short
14. Grandmotherly nickname
15. Overlook
16. "That's ___!" ("Piece of cake!")
17. Sinclair book adapted into a 1967 Disney movie, with "The"
19. Andean wool source
20. Like some frustrating traffic
21. Low-lying area
23. ___ tot
24. With 39-Across, 2007 film adapted from Sinclair's book "Oil!"
29. From an earlier era, stylistically
31. Grist for "Jeopardy!"
32. Belfry dwellers
35. Bank deposit?
37. Query from Matthew
38. Peruvian-born singer Sumac
39. See 24-Across
41. Miscalculate, say
42. Noted 1999 Daytime Emmy winner
44. Lighten
45. Some tributes
46. Italian cheese
48. "Shoot!"
50. Sinclair book adapted into a 1932 Jimmy Durante movie, with "The"
52. Raw ___ (retired Crayola color)
56. Second word of many a fairy tale
57. "Lawrence of Arabia" star Peter
58. Where hair roots grow
61. 1914 movie adapted from a 1906 Sinclair novel
64. Neighbor of Lucy and Ricky
65. Dominican-born baseball star Sammy
66. Pacers' contest?

DOWN

1. Kierkegaardian concept
2. December mall employee
3. Uppity one
4. Fools (with)
5. Boxcar rider, maybe
6. Big British record label
7. Naught
8. Jobs in the computer field?
9. It fingers ringers
10. "The Lion, the Witch, and the Wardrobe" author
11. "___ New York minute . . ."
12. "Apocalypse Now" setting, familiarly
13. 2.5 in school, e.g.
18. Grimm beast
22. It might be framed
24. Native group
25. Nation famous for tulips
26. Like the walls at Wrigley Field
27. Petrol unit
28. Villains' hideouts
30. "The Waste Land" poet's monogram
32. Corporation rule
33. Bring a smile to the face of
34. Silent
36. "We're off ___ the Wizard"
39. Gotham, with "the"
40. Poet's contraction
43. Montague rival
45. '70s singing family
47. Palacio feature
49. Costume piece in a Degas painting
51. Impatient
53. Phony
54. DeGeneres's former self-titled sitcom
55. Fishing rod attachments
57. California town east of Santa Barbara
58. "I'll be there in just a ___!"
59. Rockefeller, for one: Abbr.

67. Banana-boat box
68. Elusive Himalayan creature
69. Phishing figs.

Things Are Looking Upton

PATRICK BLINDAUER

[crossword grid]

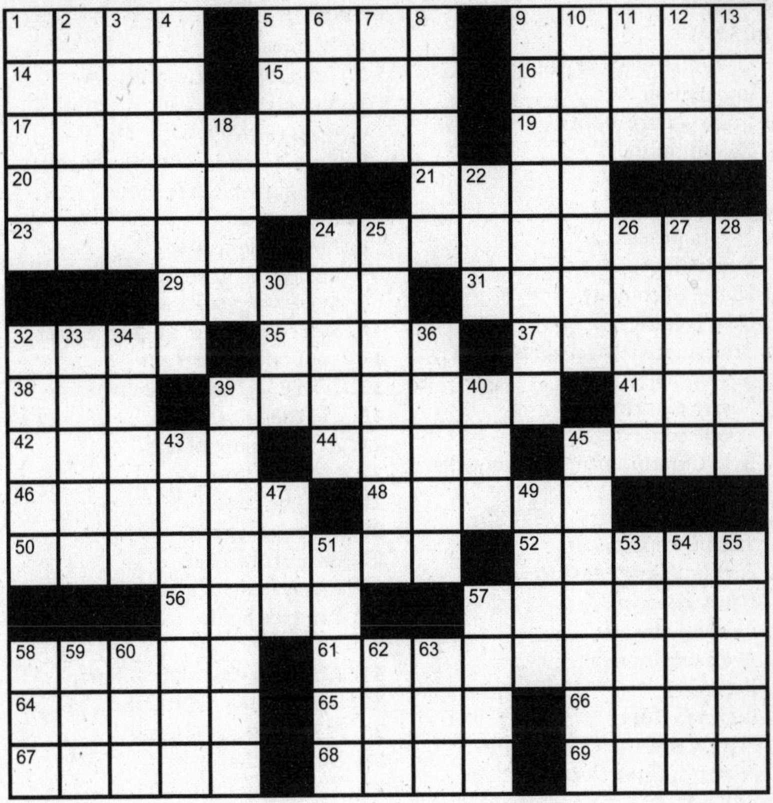

60. "Gotcha!"
62. Ground-breaking tool
63. Ballpark fig.

26

ACROSS

1. One of the five W's of journalism
5. Mine vein contents
9. "Yeah, right!"
14. Achilles, e.g.
15. All-night party
16. "___ in peace . . . "
17. Desertlike
18. Laurel of comedy
19. Dog, generically
20. Jane Austen novel about a noisy dog?
23. Not to mention
24. Simile center
25. E. E. Cummings novel about the Big Bang theory?
34. "The Cider House ___" (1985 John Irving novel)
35. Fashion designer Gucci
36. Massage locale
37. Arab chieftain
38. Available money
40. Rent-___
41. Inclined (to)
42. Hail Mary, e.g.
43. Joan ___ (French saint)
44. Edith Wharton novel about a maternity hospital?
48. Possess
49. Self-proclaimed psychic Geller
50. With 63-Across, tweaked Sue Monk Kidd title that has infiltrated the classics in this puzzle
57. "It's ___ sort of memory that only works backwards" (Carroll)
59. Capitol building feature
60. Carbon compound
61. Wandering ascetic (literally "good man" in Sanskrit)
62. Actress Cameron of "Charlie's Angels"
63. See 50-Across
64. Attack like an eagle

DOWN

1. "Kapow!"
2. Juno's Greek counterpart
3. St. Patrick's home
4. Goes to sleep, with "off"
5. Viola's love in "Twelfth Night"
6. Not quite NC-17
7. Psych. exam
8. E-mail command
9. Pablo who said, "Art is a lie that makes us realize the truth"
10. Sacred beetle of ancient Egypt
11. Toot one's horn?
12. "What ___, chopped liver?"
13. Tie the knot
21. Athletic supporters?
22. Modem units
25. Get the check
26. Skeptical grunt
27. Best of the best
28. Always, poetically
29. Parson's home
30. Vintage
31. Academy Award, familiarly
32. Eyeball-bending pictures
33. "Little Women" family
38. Nymph chasers
39. Battleship letters
40. Cinematic preservation org.
42. Get a boost, in a video game
43. Final notice?
45. Holiday syllables
46. Graham Greene's "___ in Havana"
47. Turn to ice, say
50. Big hullabaloo
51. Old Icelandic literary work
52. Dime, e.g.
53. Author Uris
54. Part of FYI, for short
55. Watch chains
56. "If all ___ fails . . . "
57. Beast of burden
58. Fido's foot

Hive Mentality

DEB AMLEN

26

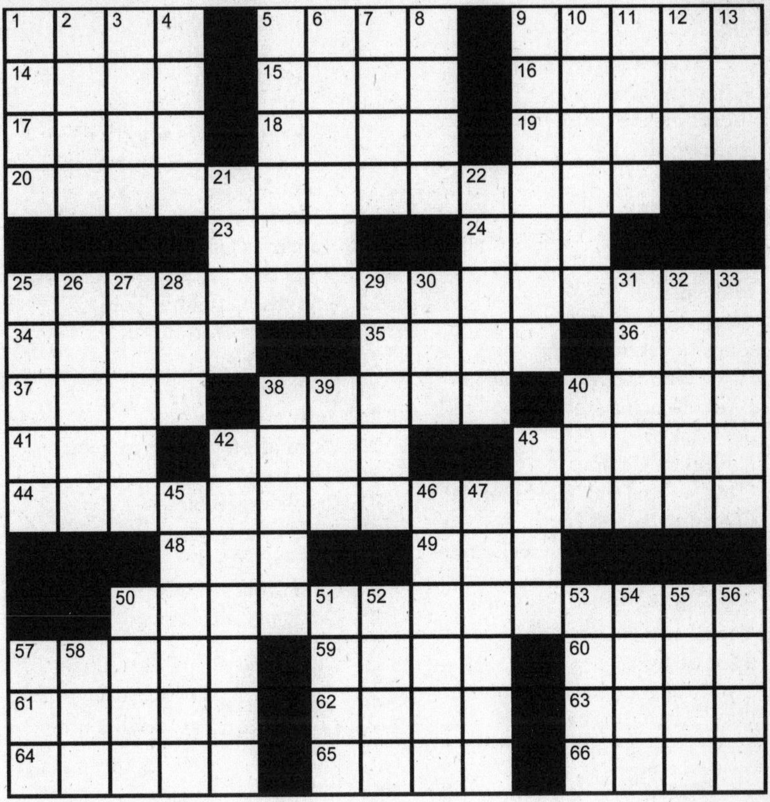

27

ACROSS

1. Sierra truck maker, for short
4. Algiers quarter
10. Words after a drum roll
14. Root word?
15. Put into battle
16. Press, as a shirt
17. Former press secretary Fleischer
18. "I swear I'll do it!"
20. Make match
22. Flock locale
23. Place to get hash, say
24. "Give War a Chance" humorist
27. Brady Bunch sister
28. Set-back area
29. Unknown element
33. "Deal or No Deal" host Mandel
36. Contend
37. Onetime Oval Office nickname
38. Elizabethan venue that burned down in 1613
43. Cookie receptacle
44. Spell badly?
45. Stroke of good luck
46. Crack at an easy target
49. Reverse or second, e.g.
51. Billy ___ Williams
52. A Beastie Boy
57. Volatile states
60. Bone in a cage
61. Jewish youth org.
62. Novel whose title characters are hidden in 18-, 24-, 38-, and 52-Across
65. Line of work, casually
66. Sacramento arena sponsor
67. One of seven U.S. states with no income tax
68. Eden woman
69. Madeline of "Clue"
70. Pint-sized
71. Like right-leaning states, on election night maps

DOWN

1. Get the gist of
2. Singer ___ Blige
3. Uniform material
4. Stereo spinners
5. Greek wind god
6. ___ of influence
7. Dickensian title adjective
8. Co. once notorious for its free CDs
9. Drum up excitement, with "up"
10. Haberdashery item
11. Silver ore
12. Something to knock on
13. Pop artist Warhol
19. Goya subject
21. Diet guru Jenny
25. European auto
26. Word often written in neon
30. "Humbug!"
31. Creole vegetable
32. Need a bath
33. URL letters
34. Kent State state
35. Got separate checks
36. Nettlwe
39. "Well, well!"
40. Early release
41. Modern place to do your bidding?
42. Lineup
47. Pulitzer-winning poet Anne
48. Foot part
49. "The Sandman" graphic novelist Neil
50. Incorporates into one's blog, as a video
53. Took the wheel
54. Burnt ___ (dark brown)
55. Popular oniony seasoning
56. Initiated, at a frat
57. Criticism
58. Euro predecessor
59. Used USPS or DHL
63. Diminutive
64. Dissenting vote

Petite Four

WILL NEDIGER

28

ACROSS

1. Scandinavian name meaning "young boy"
5. Lessened, as penalties
10. Thing to do at a meet
14. Show up
15. Moon-related
16. Leaning Tower locale
17. "It fits you to ___!"
18. Prefix with dactyl
19. Jet-black
20. Loans one scoop of mashed potatoes, e.g.?
23. One is often legal in a courthouse
24. General with a Chinese chicken dish
25. So out, it's in
28. Wearing two contacts of the same color, e.g.?
33. Resulted in
34. Film speed no.
35. Short-story master who took the middle name "Allan" after being adopted
36. Man to whom this puzzle owes a "debt" for coining 57-Across
41. Go on dates with
44. Elmer, to Bugs Bunny
45. Syrian president Bashar al-___
49. Bibliophilic entrepreneur's aspiration?
54. "The Bonfire of the Vanities" scribe Tom
55. Basketball tourney whose finals are played in MSG
56. Govt. arm at the center of a 2005 wiretapping scandal
57. Thing "present" in 20-, 28-, and 49-Across
62. Chance for change, e.g.?
64. ___ auxiliary verb (must, will, etc.)
65. Natives of Nebraska
66. Kick out of office
67. Measure taken at the wrist
68. Surfer's requirement
69. Equipment with a bell guard
70. Commit a certain traffic infraction
71. Atty.'s exam that tests logical reasoning

DOWN

1. Tool on a hospital tray
2. Be a pro around the House?
3. Fixed up, as text
4. Must-have
5. Texas city for which a salsa is named
6. Name on a spine
7. Old knife
8. ___ Grey tea
9. Fail to grasp?
10. Kind of upright piano
11. Fancy shoe
12. Pose a question
13. Settle the bill
21. Put some exclamation on the ovation
22. Mr. Glass of public radio
26. Friend of Pooh and Tigger
27. Binary code figure
29. Org. that's in the Loop?
30. "Saturday Night Fever" genre
31. Doctrine
32. "There's ___ in team!"
37. Put two and two together?
38. Rioting crowd
39. There's no accounting for it
40. FDR successor who was once a haberdasher
41. NNE's opposite
42. Help-wanted initials
43. Sun block?
46. Beethoven specialties
47. 14th-century French and Italian musical style
48. Absolutely unmovable
50. Famous
51. Reno's state: Abbr.
52. In scoring position, say
53. Frittered away, as time
58. Little troublemakers
59. French onion or Italian wedding

Make Light the Work

DAVID LIBEN-NOWELL

28

60. Sit at a traffic light
61. 1956 Allen Ginsberg poem
62. Digit with a nail that may be painted
63. Affirmative syllable

29

ACROSS

1. Hasty
5. Actress Pia who won both a Golden Globe and a Golden Raspberry for "Butterfly" (1982)
11. Prepares for some dental work
16. Spanish skating figure?
17. Erotic Ovidian opus
18. Slanting
19. Raymond Chandler crime novel about giant banana skins?
21. Bravery
22. RoboCop, for one
23. Like some intense stares
25. Swallowed
26. Etta of old comics
29. Metric prefix
30. Opening stake in cards
31. Ross Macdonald crime novel about a flood in downtown Chicago?
35. Rain omen
37. 1979 revolution nation
38. 18th-century metrosexual
39. Gabs
40. Jamie, who played a cross-dressing corporal on "M*A*S*H"
41. Bluesman ___' Mo'
42. Two-wheeled vehicle first raced at the Olympics in 2008
45. Jim Thompson crime novel about demonic possession in "The Wizard of Oz"?
49. Aerie bird
50. "Illmatic" rapper
51. "The Sea, The Sea" author Murdoch
52. "Picnic" playwright William
53. Campus e-mail ending
54. Suspense novelist Tami
55. Four-door ride
56. Agatha Christie crime novel about a sorority with sadistic hazing rituals?
61. "Avalon" band ___ Music
62. Western nickname
63. French 101 verb
64. Mohawked muscleman born Laurence Tureaud
65. Jefferson Davis was its pres.
66. Cinéma ___
71. "Invisible Cities" author Calvino
73. Graham Greene crime novel about a future war in Indochina?
78. Mountainous Asian country whose first president was sworn in on July 23, 2008
79. Pay heed
80. "Up and ___!" (catchphrase of Radioactive Man on "The Simpsons")
81. Precise
82. Stiff, as a drink
83. Sammy with 609 home runs

DOWN

1. Campus military org.
2. Sore
3. "Purple People Eater" singer Wooley
4. Train hopper, perhaps
5. Turned back quickly
6. Guitarist's equipment, for short
7. Anonymous John
8. You can dig it
9. Bill of Rights subj.
10. Birthplace of St. Clare
11. Army foe
12. Hagen of the stage
13. Pepperidge Farm cookie type
14. Three sheets to the wind
15. Child portrayer Meryl
20. Peeved
24. Sing, at the jailhouse
27. Judged events
28. "The Yankee Years" author Joe
29. Roadside resting spot
30. Mont Blanc, for one
31. Arcade currency
32. Tamale wrapper
33. Soldier
34. Asian desert
35. Cell suffix
36. Cowardly Lion portrayer Bert
40. Shows off

Final Twists

MICHAEL SHARP

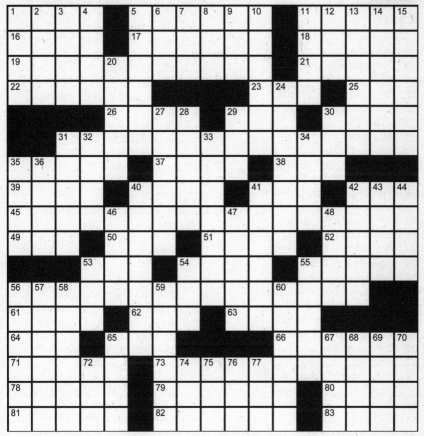

41. One named while kneeling
42. Contorts
43. Big intro?
44. Angel, Beast, Cyclops, and Marvel Girl, e.g.
46. The Dow, for short
47. Fuming
48. God, in Grenoble
53. Tarzan player Ron
54. Curse
55. Condescending facial expression
56. Stoat
57. Whirling water, e.g.
58. Popular beach resort in southern Mexico

59. Occasions for obits
60. Dr. J's last name
65. Indianapolis football player
67. Suggestions on vitamin bottles: Abbr.
68. A fan of
69. New Mexico art colony
70. Jane Austen title heroine
72. Fond du ___, Wisconsin
74. One may be pointy at a New Year's party
75. Muff it
76. Bout ender
77. Rooster's mate

30

ACROSS

1. Kept out of sight
4. Short punches
8. Throwers of TDs
11. TNT part
14. Playground challenge
16. Sch. with a Providence campus
17. River island
18. Monotony
19. Prepare to fire
20. Ronald Reagan and other linemen: Abbr.
21. Start of an Emma Goldman quote
24. Verne character Phileas
26. Lyrical Gershwin
27. Part of NRA: Abbr.
28. Second part of the quote
34. Distress signal letters
35. "___ jelly donut" (translation of "Ich Bin ein Berliner")
36. Philosopher Kierkegaard
37. Third part of the quote
40. Govt. security
42. Atmospheric prefix
43. One allowed backstage, say
46. Fourth part of the quote
50. "House" actress Ward
51. NRC forerunner
52. From square one
53. End of the quote
59. "Much ___ About Nothing"
60. Subj. of a 1972 U.S.-U.S.S.R. treaty
61. Visually acute
64. Chicago Tribune–owned superstation
65. Mens ___ (criminal intent)
66. Go all the way around
67. Bishop's domain
68. 1040, in old Rome
69. Impudent talk
70. Next of ___

DOWN

1. Towel stitching word
2. Title princess for Gilbert and Sullivan
3. One may sue for them
4. "Into the Wild" actress Malone
5. Author A.J. with "Language, Truth, and Logic"
6. Pear type
7. Japanese joint that may serve hosomaki
8. Radio wave emitter
9. Tip of the hat?
10. ___ Valley, Calif.
11. Raw steak style
12. "Amen!"
13. Emphatic pronoun
15. Japanese collaborative poetry genre
22. Provoke anger
23. Be difficult to sleep with, in a way
24. Basketball scores: Abbr.
25. ___ y plata (Montana's motto)
29. 1970s Red Sox ace Luis
30. Han's pal Calrissian in the "Star Wars" saga
31. Oft-protested global org.
32. Stars in the Roman sky
33. "Golf is a game whose aim is ___ a very small ball into an even smaller hole, with weapons singularly ill-designed for the purpose" (Churchill)
37. Indivisible substance for Leibniz
38. Food from the griddle
39. Slangy interjection of indifference
40. U2 guitarist
41. First pitch wide of the mark
43. Noted Flemish painter Jan
44. "___ had it up to here!"
45. Bench in church
46. Sounds of disbelief
47. Lion or tiger or bear
48. Triple ___
49. June of "The Dolly Sisters"
54. Hurt
55. Alpine goat

Red Emma

LEONARD WILLIAMS

56. Clinton transportation secretary Federico
57. Private eyes
58. "Last one ___ a rotten egg!"
62. Biblical judge
63. Hibernation place

31

ACROSS

1. Demean
6. "Dancing Queen" group
10. Getting 100 percent on, say
15. "Chill!"
16. Viscount's superior
17. Infielder Garciaparra whose name is his father's spelled backward
18. ___ for the mill
19. Hook's henchman
20. Post-coup ruling group
21. Book about beatniks tripping through Winston-Salem? (Kerouac/Caldwell)
24. Thing collected from a deadbeat
25. Take stock?
26. Deity once worshipped at the Parthenon
30. Seep through gradually
33. Dinero
34. Empire whose capital was at Tenochtitlán
35. Rolled-up newspaper sound
39. Book about Barbie's depressing digs? (Ibsen/Dickens)
42. Native Arizonan
43. "There's ___ in sight"
44. Instrument for The Doors
45. "In Search of Lost Time" author
47. Broken, as promises
48. Lift to the top of a mountain
51. Maine local color author Sarah ___ Jewett
53. Book about a global exposition of narcissism? (Thackeray/Doctorow)
60. "Sappho's Leap" author Jong
61. Great Lakes canal
62. Trunk
63. Pester
64. Briny bodies
65. Real estate encumbrances
66. Got to second base, maybe
67. Scads
68. Poet with the line "That is no country for old men"

DOWN

1. Jason's conveyance
2. Swiss city where Einstein devised the theory of relativity
3. Landed
4. Pageant adornment
5. Not on the inside
6. Man of morals
7. Hoodwinks
8. La ___ Tar Pits
9. Jack's portrayer on "30 Rock"
10. Alternatives to Boscs and Bartletts
11. Classes
12. "___ kidding here!"
13. Of birth
14. C+, e.g.
22. Afternoon cupful
23. Stewpot
26. East Asian nanny
27. Errand list heading
28. Earring shape
29. ___ machine (treadmill alternative)
31. Booming, as a voice
32. Man-made lake formed by Hoover Dam
34. "___ Ben Adhem" (James Leigh Hunt poem)
36. Titanic
37. PDQ
38. Cooped (up)
40. Coming down outside, in winter
41. "Some people!"
46. Take turns, literally or figuratively
47. Sturm ___ Drang
48. Many Scandinavian males
49. Purity measure for diamonds
50. "Hello, my name is ___ Montoya. You killed my father. Prepare to die."
52. Like May through August, letterwise
54. Left, on a map

Strange Bookfellows

JOON PAHK

55. Source of twisted pleasure at dessert?
56. Pâté de ___ gras
57. Bailiwick
58. Exists no more
59. Diana of the Supremes

32

ACROSS

1. Use the shower, say
6. Bread at an Indian restaurant
10. "Germinal" author Émile
14. Grammy Award-winning Mark
15. "How to Lose ___ in 10 Days"
16. Steinbeck title locale
17. *Courters of 27-Across
19. Long-distance swimmer Diana
20. Venezuelan MLBer Melvin
21. Frat party outfit
22. Hindu seer
23. Fragrances
25. Hits, runs, and steals
27. *Steadfast love of 11-Down
30. *Patron goddess of 11-Down
33. Makes many demands
35. Swiss canton
36. Aquarium clapper
39. Zeta follower
40. Ivan the Terrible, e.g.
41. Fast-food chain, commonly
42. Strange
46. *Island where 27-Across and 11-Down live
48. *Major challenger of 11-Down
52. Ready to bloom
54. Wipe out
55. Commits a foul, on a pinball machine
57. Broccoli ___
60. PC exit keys
61. Caramel candy brand
62. *Man of the house, while 11-Down is away
64. Bremner of "Trainspotting"
65. Pro___ (proportionally)
66. Cheri, formerly of "Saturday Night Live"
67. Leisurely
68. Love, to Ovid
69. "The Cider House Rules" director Hallström

DOWN

1. Image file format
2. On land
3. "Monster" star Charlize
4. Breaks the fast, perhaps
5. Largest bird native to Australia
6. Intl. alliance since 1949
7. Highly excited
8. Vibes
9. Albany is its cap.
10. Korean HDTV maker
11. *Weary traveler of literature
12. Laban's daughter, in the Bible
13. "The King ___ "
18. "No problem!"
22. Hair metal band with "Round and Round"
24. "Happy Days" hangout
26. Asian "way"
28. Minute div.
29. Consume rabidly
31. Gun lobby org.
32. Melody
34. Composer Schifrin
36. Hope for good powder, perhaps
37. Young salamander
38. *Warrior recruited by 11-Down
40. Racetrack betting option
42. Banned chemicals
43. Mer material
44. "___ to recall . . ."
45. Pershing's WWI command
47. Cleopatra's gent
49. "Mad" runs
50. Happens
51. Loch dweller of legend
53. Freudian interpretation
55. Arboretum study
56. Ames Straw Poll state
58. Choir voice
59. Grizzly, e.g.
62. La-la intro
63. Popular ISP

Long Time Passing

VIVIAN COLLINS

33

ACROSS

1. Hand-dyeing technique
6. Fido's fare
10. Likely to spare the rod
14. Suspect's story
15. Prepare, as pasta
16. Like the driven snow
17. Irish author of "Finnegans Wake"
19. Heaps and heaps
20. Actress Sue ___ Langdon
21. Scotch partner
22. Crop up
23. Irish author of "Waiting for Godot"
27. Great artist, say
29. "The ___ Man and the Sea"
30. "QB VII" author Leon
31. Irish author of "Juno and the Paycock"
38. Pricey balcony seating
39. LBJ successor
40. Start of a 1957 Harry Belafonte hit
41. Irish author of "The Country Girls"
45. Of all time
46. Performing pair
47. Counter
49. Irish author of "The Informer"
55. Nobel Peace Prize winner ___ el-Sadat
56. French Polynesian atoll
57. Feel under the weather
60. Bed board
61. Irish author of "The Picture of Dorian Gray"
64. Drink with sashimi
65. Felt bad about
66. MacBook maker
67. Came up short
68. Less appealing bread pieces, perhaps
69. American Beauties, e.g.

DOWN

1. Mexicali's locale, for short
2. Arkin of "Glengarry Glen Ross"
3. It makes multiples
4. "When Will ___ Loved?" (Everly Brothers song)
5. Passionate request
6. Humble home
7. Far from fickle
8. Snap
9. Pamplona plaudit
10. Mutual attraction
11. Certain belly button
12. "The Road Not Taken" poet
13. Religious principle
18. Nice days?
22. "For Those About to Rock We Salute You" band
24. Clueless
25. "___ chance!"
26. Self-titled 1971 progressive rock album
27. Stubborn sort
28. Yankee who plays next to Jeter, to fans
32. Flynn of "The Sun Also Rises"
33. "___ missing something?"
34. More than capable
35. Mont Blanc's range
36. Sight seers?
37. Long ago
42. Secret target?
43. The Bills, on an NFL scoreboard
44. Lack of musical talent
48. Like a hawk
49. Roundup rope
50. Acquired relative
51. Up
52. Paired up, in a way
53. Like parabolas
54. Toss selection
58. Twiddling one's thumbs
59. Wine dregs
61. Bauxite or magnetite
62. It may have spots
63. Wall St. debut

Eire of Reading

NANCY SALOMON

34

DOWN

1. State abbr.
2. ___ carte
3. GPS reading
4. Campus antiwar gp. of the '60s
5. Dino, for the Flintstones
6. Shapeless pond dweller
7. Steamy
8. MADD concern
9. "Howdy!"
10. Steer clear of
11. 1996 Olympian Strug who landed her vault on an injured ankle
12. Thus far
14. Password's partner
18. Friends of Sartre and Camus?
19. Like many old first editions
23. Takes a spill
24. Came about
25. Eyelid nuisance
26. Trepidation
30. NYC summer hrs.
33. Comic book noise
35. Vacant, as a house
36. Mania
37. Champing at the bit
39. Where the "Madagascar" stars escaped from
40. Bollywood dress
41. Office honcho
44. "OK, I've had enough!"
46. Totally surprises
48. Class pres., maybe
49. Beat at a track meet, say
51. Alan who won acting, writing, and directing Emmys for "M*A*S*H"
52. French composer Erik of "Gymnopédies"
53. Loathe
54. Actress Davis of "Thelma & Louise"
56. Inscribed pillar
61. Italian writer Umberto
62. You'll get a bang out of it
63. Cooking fuel

ACROSS

1. Indian lentil dish
4. Tiff
8. Bangladeshi city called the rickshaw capital of the world
13. Multi-generational baseball family name
15. Customer's how-to preview
16. Shakespeare's merry ones
17. Area carved out of the Louisiana Purchase in 1854
20. Superb specimen
21. It's measured by the cup
22. Provide with a gig
23. "You had a chance, so I should get one, too!"
27. Tweak, as a manuscript
28. Montmartre frequenter, say
29. Rawlings's yearling, for one
31. Raucous
32. Jabber
34. Tie on the court
38. "The Electric Kool-Aid Acid Test" acid
39. Math grouping that contains nothing?
42. Bunch of big-gun lobbyists?
43. Take care of
45. Ear clogger
46. Patriotic symbol
47. Dust Bowl wanderer
50. Come to understand
52. Story of the Forsytes, e.g.
55. Regular concertgoer, perhaps
57. Assist unadvisedly
58. Hall of Famer Mel
59. Mama rabbit
60. Children's classic about an orphan and her sickly cousin, and a hint to the circled words
66. Like some Greek columns
67. Elbow-to-wrist bone
68. Hindu "Destroyer"
69. Ovid's muse
70. Crab nabbers

In Bloom

LYNN LEMPEL

(crossword grid, puzzle 34)

64. "All About ___"
65. Pester over and over and over

35

ACROSS

1. Weirdo
6. "A ___ Wanted Man" (John le Carré)
10. Old World cont.
13. Guilty statement
15. Arizona county
16. Palindromic name in old Hollywood
17. Samuel Taylor Coleridge's fictional place
18. Jonathan Swift's fictional place
20. LAN part
22. Where enfants are educated
23. Lake, to Luigi
27. Evelyn Waugh's fictional place
30. Samuel Butler's fictional place
32. Suffix with percent
33. Heavy metric weight
34. Gagging sound
35. Mexican supermodel Benítez
39. Aristophanes' fictional place
43. Whole bunch
44. Pale ___
45. Polynesian country that exports many coconut products
46. Take for a fool
47. F. Scott Fitzgerald's fictional place
49. Thomas Hardy's fictional place
54. Hebrides dialect
55. One with a fiery demeanor, astrologically
56. "The best ___ schemes o' mice an' men / Gang aft agley"
58. Kenneth Grahame's fictional place
61. Margaret Atwood's fictional place
66. "To Serve ___" (classic "Twilight Zone" episode)
67. City in Ventura County
68. Shag, for instance
69. Denver-to-Des Moines dir.
70. 1961 Elie Wiesel novel
71. Possess without owning

DOWN

1. Make unfair, as an election
2. Nutritional initials
3. Un : France :: ___ : Germany
4. Nabokov novel set on Antiterra
5. Radiohead album that was promoted with video "blips"
6. Site of a tragedy exposed by Seymour Hersh
7. Si, in Paris
8. T-shirt size option letters
9. "Unto the Sons" author
10. "The Raven" writer, in footnotes
11. Vibrator in the throat
12. Given a G, say
14. Like some sports car engines
19. I, in Vienna
21. Sea eagle
23. Creep, slangily
24. Play ___ (do something significant)
25. Columbus's birthplace
26. Confess (to)
28. Gumshoe
29. Nevada's second-largest county
31. Terri Clark's "I Wish ___ Been Drinkin' Whiskey"
34. Unreturnable serve, say
35. Delight
36. Less believable, as an excuse
37. Makes out, in Britain
38. "Love conquers all," e.g.
40. Johnny nicknamed "the man in black"
41. "___'s Gold"
42. CIA antecedent
46. Like wild horses
47. Pilot's guesstimate: Abbr.
48. On ___ (feeling great)
49. Wonderland cake message
50. Pun response, perhaps
51. Photographer Arbus
52. Heavy ref. work
53. One way for a confident poker player to go
57. Archaic phone feature

Unreal Estate

BRENDAN EMMETT QUIGLEY

1	2	3	4	5		6	7	8	9		10	11	12
13				14		15					16		
17						18			19				
			20		21			22					
23	24	25	26		27			28	29				
30			31				32						
33						34				35	36	37	38
39			40	41				42					
43			44				45						
		46			47	48							
49	50	51	52			53				54			
55						56		57					
58			59	60			61		62	63	64	65
66			67				68						
69			70					71					

59. Steely Dan's first Grammy-winning album

60. You may follow the letter or the spirit of it

62. Tell a story

63. Any president's time in office, e.g.

64. Output of the fictional TV office Sterling Cooper

65. Anonymous name

36

ACROSS

1. Thing refused by the three authors in this puzzle's theme
6. Convalescing, perhaps
9. Franciscan friar Junipero who founded several missions in California
14. New version of an old song, perhaps
15. Foot digit
16. Sewing machine innovator Howe
17. Egg-shaped
18. Essayist Michel de ___
20. *1958 Nobel (pressure from the Soviet government)
22. Squeeze (out)
23. Notable feature of cyclops
24. Nova ___
26. Attacks
29. Multitude
30. Traffic cone color
34. ___ Dinh Diem, first president of South Vietnam
35. *1926 Pulitzer (displeasure at the Pulitzer standards)
40. Scornful word
41. Runs, as colors
42. Asimov short-story collection
46. Sizzling Tex-Mex entrée
50. Elaborate bank heists, for example
51. Caged jailbird who sings?
53. Macadamia or cashew
54. *1964 Nobel (saying "a writer must refuse to allow himself to be transformed into an institution")
58. One-hundredth of a lira
59. Hotelier Helmsley who willed her dog $12 million
60. To have, in Rouen
61. Homer Simpson's annoyed grunt
62. Cons, in a debate
63. A little crazy
64. Victorian ___

DOWN

1. Congressional inquiries
2. Take back
3. Ankara inn
4. Pasta choice
5. Former flames
6. "Be that as ___ . . ."
7. Like old pants after a diet
8. Time of abstemiousness
9. Google, as a verb
10. One of the two heroines in "Sense and Sensibility"
11. Alternative to 4-Down
12. Specialty of U.S. News & World Report
13. Enzyme suffix
19. King Lear puts his daughters through one at the beginning of the play
21. She loves me . . . she loves me not discard
25. Long, long ___
27. Biff Loman, to Willy
28. Rainbow shape
31. Apprehend
32. ___ Blas (18th-century French picaresque novel)
33. Before, to Marlowe
35. Balkan city that hosted the 1988 Winter Olympics
36. "Heaven forbid!"
37. Half of a boxer's repertoire, perhaps
38. Author LeShan who hosted "How Do Your Children Grow" on PBS
39. Financial Times rival, in brief
40. Ballpoint pen brand
43. Michael Jackson tune that replaced "Come On Eileen" as Billboard's #1 song
44. Cantankerous
45. Julia Child's measurements: Abbr.
47. Overall
48. Hit the hay

Thanks, but No Thanks

MATT MATERA

49. Opposite of "Ten-hut!"
51. Fruit of the vine?
52. Hawaii, the ___ State
55. Professor's helper
56. Former Fed chief Greenspan
57. "The Biggest Little City in the World"
58. Heel

37

ACROSS

1. Little white lie
4. Persnickety
10. Something a toddler might go through
15. White Monopoly bill
16. Lens cover, in the eye
17. "A Doll's House" playwright
18. V times XIX
19. Shower accessories
20. Tag line?
21. With 62-Across, locale in the most famous section of 40-Across
24. Israeli gun in many action movies
25. Prefix with space
26. Miss the mark
27. Pearl harborer
29. "The Portrait of a Lady" lady Archer
32. Shed skin
34. Give up, as land
35. Schlep
36. Pulitzer playwright Akins
38. The N in TNT
40. Musical works based on a play by 17-Across
45. Signatory to New Zealand's Treaty of Waitangi
46. Jackson 5 hit
47. Work week starter, on a cal.
49. Fake
52. Bottle part named for a body part
54. Holy place
56. "We ___!" ("We reached the end!")
58. Laotian money
60. Move lightly
61. Gold, in Granada
62. See 21-Across
66. Sacred Rastafarian herb
68. Muhammad's daughter
69. In the style of

70. 40-Across composer
71. Some fraternity members
72. Hanoi Hilton locale
73. Kind of question
74. Philosopher implicated in the Pisonian conspiracy
75. Be short, monetarily

DOWN

1. Grass cluster
2. Increases slowly
3. Host's offering
4. Pac-10 univ.
5. Hustler's game
6. "Nineteen Eighty-Four" worker
7. Tell
8. Resort spot, say
9. "And ___ thou slain the Jabberwock?"
10. Like some air fresheners
11. "Curb Your Enthusiasm" network
12. Discerning
13. Took by force
14. Not missing anything
22. Prefix with goblin
23. Backyard party locales
28. Kilt wearer
30. Book after II Chronicles
31. Access, as a site
33. Saxophone-playing character Simpson
37. Fictional orphan raised at Gateshead
39. Full of calories, probably
41. One-named supermodel
42. Sobriquet
43. Mexican revolutionary Zapata
44. New kin after a wedding
48. Obsolescent tennis style
49. Polluted, as the air above a highway
50. Zimbabwe's capital
51. Handsome fellow
53. Mewing litter member
55. Washington, D.C.'s ___ Stadium
57. Adult insect
59. Satchel in Cooperstown
63. "National Enquirer" subjects
64. Apple variety

What's the Score?

WILL NEDIGER

65. Hubble telescope org.
67. Actress Aniston, familiarly

38

ACROSS

1. With 64-Across, where the answers to the starred clues appear in their respective books
6. Quick haircut
10. Market index, with "the"
13. Vertical, as an anchor on the bottom
14. Maltreat
15. "I believe," in chat-room shorthand
16. *"The Metamorphosis" character
18. Oslo's land: Abbr.
19. Abates
20. Auto amenity
22. "Science Guy" Bill
23. Plural suffix
25. Somme summers
26. *"V" character
31. Women's tapered trousers
34. More, in Mexico
35. Regretful sort
36. Wanted poster info
37. There are 2.2 in a kg.
38. Popular kitchen wrap brand
39. Campus marchers
40. Brouhaha
41. San Luis ___, California
42. *"Ulysses" character
45. Successor
46. Andy Samberg's show, for short
47. Mixed vaccine, briefly
50. Great film, in critic-speak
53. Carrier of an afternoon spot?
56. Mount St. Helens output
57. *"The Fountainhead" character
59. Italian race car driver Fabi
60. Bygone Olds model
61. Crop up
62. Gallery filler
63. Job benefit
64. See 1-Across

DOWN

1. Donald of Steely Dan
2. Starting words of a supplication
3. Witherspoon of "Legally Blonde"
4. Herb that tastes amazing sauteed in butter
5. Fight enders, briefly
6. TV Guide abbr.
7. Bacardi products
8. Companies selling stock, e.g.
9. Treating unkindly
10. Bird relatives, according to some scientists
11. Melville's Tahiti novel
12. Klingon on a starship
14. Poplar variety
17. Archaeologist's venue
21. "Lucy in the sky with diamonds," e.g.
24. Characters, say
26. Income level, to the IRS
27. Autobahn hazard
28. Sound systems, for short
29. Twice-monthly tide
30. Mechanical puzzle maker Rubik
31. Engine part, briefly
32. Matty, Moises, or Felipe of baseball
33. Way out of a trap?
37. "Bad" cholesterol letters
38. Start-up co. helper
40. Ring of light
41. Looked at lustfully
43. Accident
44. First song on an album, perhaps
47. Run through a colander
48. Break down, as a sentence
49. Small fries
50. ___ Hari
51. Manipulative sort
52. Decorative pitcher with a base
54. Uzbekistan border sea
55. Amos or Spelling
58. Cruise for couples?

From the Top

PANCHO HARRISON

39

ACROSS

1. Puncture
5. Playwright Karel who coined the term "robot"
10. "The Apple Cart" penner, 1929
14. E. ___ (rod-shaped bacteria)
15. Common typeface
16. Guadalajara greeting
17. Goes (for)
18. Like church matters
20. Yellowed copy of a 1933 John Steinbeck novella?
22. Bodega meat
23. Depot: Abbr.
24. Post-grad deg.
27. Abbr. after Brooklyn or Cleveland
28. Take acid, say
32. Mississippi stomping ground of William Faulkner
34. Union contract?
36. "Night" author Wiesel
37. Yellowed copy of an 1873 Thomas Hardy novel, with "A"?
42. Verdi heroine
43. Bakery by-products
44. Mechanical malfunction
47. Leave off, as an all-star team
48. Wind dir.
51. "___ Beso"
52. Get on one's knees, say
54. Census option
56. Yellowed copy of a 1982 Alice Walker novel?
61. "The Name of the Rose" author
63. The E in HOMES
64. Part of the mouth where a "ch" sound is made
65. Where Hemingway committed suicide
66. Longings
67. Sequential word
68. Benjamin, so to speak
69. Certain NCO

DOWN

1. Potent potable that's the subject of a Robert Burns poem
2. Part of Mr. Peanut's outfit
3. Changes, as the ending
4. Buffalo relative
5. Biblical marriage site
6. Elvis's middle name, sometimes
7. Sonar sound
8. Lightens (up)
9. One who likes things hot?
10. Give the cold shoulder to
11. "Jumpin' Jehoshaphat!"
12. ___ mode (menu phrase)
13. "For Whom the Bell Tolls" subject
19. Talk into
21. Like lava lamps, now
25. Soft French cheese
26. Fruity quenchers
29. Soccer official
30. TV's Swenson
31. Appreciates the petting, perhaps
33. Membership requirements
34. Backside, slangily
35. Lowly employee
37. Book leaf
38. Has a bug
39. Tube, pejoratively
40. Outback meat source
41. Head honcho
45. "Smokey" spotter on the road
46. Lacking organization
48. Maritime edges
49. Quaint hobby
50. Oscar winner Borgnine
53. Services' partner?
55. Three-pointers, in basketball slang
57. Weight
58. "Look before you ___"
59. Huit, across the Pyrenees
60. Diplomat Elihu
61. Tea vessel
62. Stooge Howard

Showing Some Age

ANDREW RIES

40

ACROSS

1. Work
6. Worry
10. Rikki-Tikki-___ (Kipling character)
14. Cutting edge?
15. Swearing-in statement
16. Take way too much of, briefly
17. Poet with "Are You Not Weary of Ardent Ways" (via Stephen Dedalus)
19. High-end stereo maker
20. Basic abodes
21. Super Bowl XLI champions
22. Without exception
26. Thread-cutting Fate
28. Poet with "The Waking"
30. Prevails
31. Legal records
32. Poet with "Do Not Go Gentle Into That Good Night"
38. Home of the philosopher Zeno
39. Mother of Helen, Clytemnestra, Castor, and Pollux
42. Poet with "One Art"
49. Grail finder of legend
50. Weapons maker
51. Large swallows?
52. Hydrox look-alike
53. Short cut?
54. Nineteen-line verse form for the poems in this puzzle's theme
60. Affliction for the Squeaky-Voiced Teen on "The Simpsons"
61. French notion
62. Nunavut native
63. Berated, old-style
64. Digital camera feature
65. One of Ben Franklin's "certainties in life"

DOWN

1. Monogram of four concurrent White House inhabitants
2. Chicken ___ king
3. Emeril catchphrase
4. "Dejection: An ___" (Coleridge poem)
5. Given new sandals, say
6. Header's counterpart
7. Emanations from the sun
8. "And so on and so forth . . ."
9. With 26-Down, Eero Saarinen masterpiece, informally
10. On top of everything
11. Former New York Times owner Ochs
12. ___ 1 (space mission for Yuri Gagarin)
13. Really, legally
18. 2007 title role for Ellen Page
21. Prepare for baking, as butter
22. 36-Down, in a text message
23. Pacific yellowfin tuna
24. "___ your hearts, not your garments" (Joel 2:13)
25. Overly inquisitive
26. See 9-Down
27. Oz canine
29. Patronize, as a diner
33. Jacob's first wife, et al.
34. Jessica of "Dark Angel"
35. No mere luxury
36. "One more thing . . ."
37. "___ gut!" (German compliment)
40. Last name in anonymity
41. Fools' Day mo.
42. Spider's hatching milieu
43. Get off the ground, as a rocket
44. The Big 10's Fighting ___
45. Used a phaser on, say
46. ___ Renaissance (movement for Langston Hughes and Jean Toomer)
47. Tar, in Spanish
48. "Leave this to me"
52. Butter alternative
54. Relative of "i.e."
55. Words uttered at the altar
56. Bambi's aunt
57. "___ et veritas" (Yale motto)
58. Tell a whopper
59. GRE company

Nineteen Lines

JOON PAHK

40

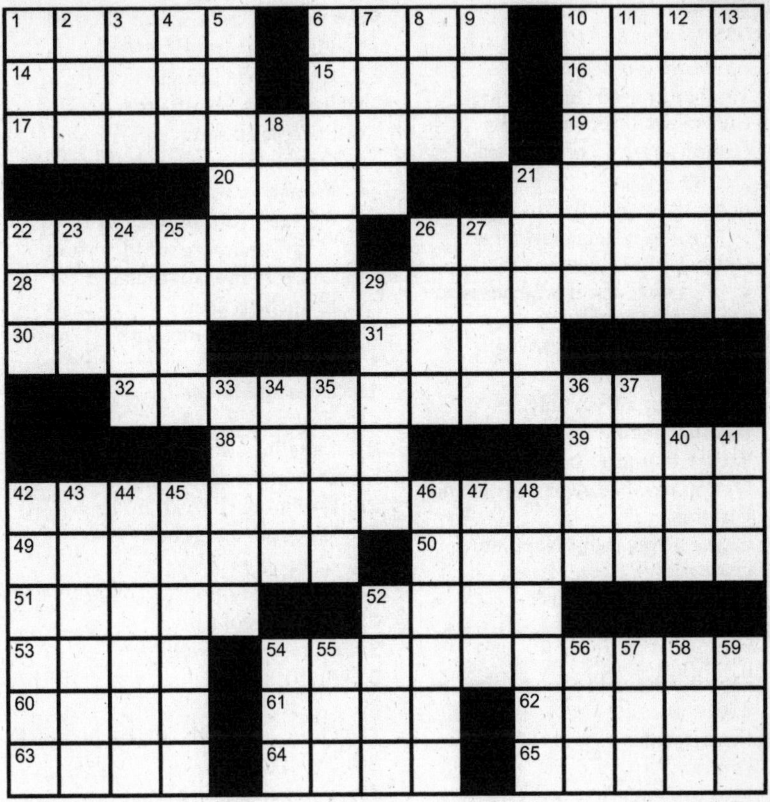

41

ACROSS

1. Egyptian crosses
6. 1998 animated flick featuring the voice of Woody Allen
10. Campus area
14. Vestige
15. Liver, in Lyon
16. ___ Reader (alternative news source)
17. Crime novel about a father who remarries again?
19. "Must've been something ___"
20. German pronoun
21. Change for a five, maybe
22. Debauched one
24. Father-daughter boxing pair
25. NYC mayor between Beame and Dinkins
26. Crime novel about Napoleon's last days?
31. Old quarterback Bart
33. None
34. None
35. Jay who moved to prime time in 2009
36. Ostentatious
38. Yank
39. Play someone
40. Grumble
41. They may be shown to novices
42. Crime novel about an undercover aristocrat?
46. Distort
47. Rice-A-___
48. Corn- or flour-based wrap
51. Feeling, in slang
52. Motor homes, in brief
55. "Pronto!"
56. Crime novel about a widespread leak?
59. Gin and tonic citrus
60. Ireland, to the Irish
61. Upper-crust people
62. Mad scientists' locales
63. Places for facials
64. Holy council

DOWN

1. Fine or liberal follower
2. Grape soda brand
3. Paul of the Bauhaus school
4. Successful song
5. One with research credentials
6. From the top
7. Agrees without saying a word
8. "Tiny" character of literature
9. Too-fervent fanaticism
10. Brunch choice
11. Birthplace of Roseanne Barr
12. Forced bet
13. Does and bucks
18. "Put a sock ___"
23. Canyon sound effect
24. Dynamic beginning?
25. Had more than an inkling
26. He wrote about hell
27. Atmospheric layer
28. Possessed of butterfingers, say
29. Milan moola, once
30. Some lodge dwellers
31. Blinds piece
32. ___ support
36. Philosopher who drank hemlock
37. Dwell (on)
38. Mitchell of song
40. Chicken or turkey, e.g.
41. Goes back (on)
43. Uses a credit card, say
44. People with reservations
45. Desert near Beijing
48. Go down
49. Burma's continent
50. Door feature
51. Aloe ___
52. Jockey's handful
53. Presidential power
54. Did 50 in a 45, say
57. With it
58. Soul singer Stone

The Purloined Letter

JOHN CUNNINGHAM

42

ACROSS

1. Handkerchief-dropping Shakespeare villain
5. Pet adoption agcy.
9. Make embarrassed
14. Gloppy mass
15. Gator's cousin
16. Old-looking photo tint
17. Wintry weather forecast?
19. Nose ticklers
20. "Bye for now"
21. TV dial letters
23. Permit to
24. Time when things just aren't going right
27. Top-notch
28. Asset for a double play combo?
33. Last stop for Iditarod mushers
34. Cowboys' stats
35. Coauthor of the "Communist Manifesto"
38. Pause indicator
40. Make a choice
42. Preemptive shout before tag begins
43. Looking like rain, perhaps
45. Org. to get you going?
47. Peruvian coastal city
48. Task for the breakfast chef?
51. "The Naked and the Dead" enemy
53. Really great joke
54. Ann Patchett's "___ Canto"
55. Faux follower
56. Daytona 500 overseer
61. Like Yeats and Bono, ethnically
63. Robust farm baby?
66. Nodded off
67. Sicilian volcano
68. Climactic beginning?
69. Bigwigs at the office
70. High places?
71. Jumbled state

DOWN

1. Some early PCs
2. Natural burn soother
3. Peace Nobelist Al of 2007
4. Toe the line
5. Unkempt
6. Major leaguer, say
7. Trig. ratio
8. Honest-to-goodness
9. Up to
10. Word before rock or roll
11. Contrite
12. Odysseus's singing temptress
13. Alacrity
18. Cover, as the bill
22. Literary alter ego
25. Common kennel name
26. Utter hopelessness
27. Noted Louisiana penitentiary
28. 1960s civil rights gp.
29. Result of a fleecing
30. Freeze, in a way
31. Long leg bones
32. The Admiral Benbow, for one
36. Common prom wheels
37. "South Park" kid
39. Fuss
41. Take a nosedive
44. Girls' rec. center
46. They may be handed out at the beginning of meetings
49. Raids the fridge, maybe
50. Petting zoo sound
51. Tolerate
52. Company whose name is a verb for what its machines do
55. Most profs
57. Take down, as in wrestling
58. Walker's aid
59. Rx dosages, e.g.
60. Homer's earnings, briefly?
62. "Just a ___!" ("Hold on!")
64. Had brunch, say
65. Protein-making cell substance

Classic Couples

LYNN LEMPEL

43

ACROSS

1. Bison baby
5. Pep (up)
10. Is, to Isabella
14. Woodwind section member
15. Dote on
16. For each
17. *Subordinate trial venue
19. Hotel room posting
20. Thomas Gray's "The Bard," e.g.
21. Is bedridden, perhaps
22. Pained facial reactions
24. Makes bigger, say, with Photoshop
26. Blakley of "Nashville"
27. Many a Christmas tree
28. "___ Park" (Crichton thriller)
31. "Three Lives" author Gertrude
34. Allen who created "Candid Camera"
35. Bolshoi skirt
36. Wizened witch
37. Happen as planned
40. Defrosting target
41. Physics units
43. Sucking appliances, briefly
44. They're sworn
46. Opera on which "Rent" is based
48. Protective sports equipment
49. Blazing
50. Vanishing craft
54. Keeps moist, as a turkey in the oven
56. Pull a fast one on
57. ___ Day (Hawaiian festival)
58. Yoda's trainee
59. *Writing tool bearing a 4, say
62. Nod was east of it
63. Inedible orange
64. Stick together
65. Smart people may match them
66. Fragrant compound

DOWN

67. Matter for Sherlock, or word that can follow either half of the answers to this puzzle's starred clues

1. "The ___ Purple" (Alice Walker book)
2. Dwelling
3. Home-improvement chain
4. Doctor's due
5. Having more frilly trim
6. Winners on a popular musical talent show
7. S'il ___ plaît
8. Misspeak or misspell
9. Post-expenses value
10. "The Importance of Being ___"
11. *Apollo apparel
12. Spacious bag
13. Primatologist's study
18. Bringing to the ground
23. "Never ___ million years!"
25. "___ Ruled the World"
26. Symbolic steps toward success
28. Lemon liquid
29. Urge
30. Stage alerts
31. Silverstein who wrote Johnny Cash's "A Boy Named Sue"
32. Reid of "The Big Lebowski"
33. *Henhouse container
34. Wrongly accuse
38. Rainy day footwear
39. Ruffle, as hair
42. Makes less incendiary
45. Well-put
47. Hightail it
48. Barrel maker
50. Elks faction
51. Big brand in aluminum
52. Horse rider's handful
53. Something to go over jalapeños?
54. Botched completely
55. German sports car maker
56. Collegiate clique, for short
60. Donkey ancestor
61. Network with "Friends" and "Frasier"

Holmes Brew

PATRICK JORDAN

44

ACROSS

1. Icy precipitation
5. Biology class letters
8. Fine spray
12. Cube maker Rubik
13. Prefix meaning "totally"
14. Greenwich, CT, neighborhood home to a former impressionist art colony
16. *Joseph Conrad novel subtitled "A Tale of the Seaboard"
18. *Sir Walter Scott novel with a Scottish folk hero
19. Home city to Montana Tech
20. Wingtip or loafer
22. "Have a ___ day!"
23. Enzyme ending
24. Fencer's warning
27. Mail repository with a key: Abbr.
28. In an organized way
30. *"War and Peace" novelist
32. Whirlpool
33. In ___ (effectively)
36. Grocery store division
37. *With "The," play by Plautus originally titled "Aulularia"
40. Scoffing sort
43. Rich soil
44. Sea eagles
48. *Ivan Goncharov title character who fails to leave his bed in the first 150 pages
50. Don't be so hard (on)
52. Summer sign
53. Time to see the stars
56. Metro stop: Abbr.
57. Cigar tip?
59. Playwright Bogosian
60. Consumed
62. *Author Dostoevsky . . .
64. *. . . and the title of his first novel
66. Stereotypical street gang members
67. Shaker founder Lee
68. Perry Mason creator ___ Stanley Gardner
69. Western Athletic Conference athletes
70. Gp. that regulates carry-on luggage
71. Don, as clothes

DOWN

1. Plant also called stinking nightshade
2. Excited
3. As an alternative
4. Trent late of the Senate
5. P, in the Greek alphabet
6. Chinese restaurant disclaimer
7. Greeting while offering a lei
8. Holstein noise
9. Bar code on a book
10. Cast handouts
11. "That's sooo great!"
14. Set of beliefs
15. "See ya later"
17. Rod attachment
21. Big name in Mexican food products
25. No, to Nicholas II
26. Airline to Jerusalem
29. Like blood that can be universally donated
31. Hexagon's six, e.g.
34. You, of this puzzle
35. California airport, on luggage tags
38. "Coffee, Tea, ___?"
39. It's a sign
40. Hang a louie
41. Start of a certain dare
42. Obscure, visually
45. Fix up, as furniture
46. Hazelnut spread brand
47. Naughty-sounding schooner sail nearest the stern
49. Voice-___ (commercial narrations)
51. Teen follower?
54. Bite playfully
55. Desktop symbols

The Marquise of O

MATT JONES

58. Starting point of many jigsaw puzzles
61. Some
63. "I just got it" noises
65. "Cat ___ Hot Tin Roof"

45

ACROSS

1. Nightclub in a Manilow song
5. Openly gay
8. Noncom nickname
13. ___ even keel
14. Overly passionate person
17. Monotheistic belief system, usually
19. "Laughing" scavenger
20. Certain hosp. employee
21. Test for future M.A.'s
22. Celebrity's entourage
23. Make mention of, in a paper
25. Swenson of "Benson"
26. Director's yell
27. Coral groups
29. Cheated, slangily
30. Poker Flat chronicler Harte
32. Ruckus
33. Tend, as the lawn
34. School cafeteria entrée, facetiously
38. Geometry symbols
39. Something to chew on
40. Transplanter's purchase
43. Scent sensors
46. Ship wheels
48. Mo. for buying masks
49. Quito's land: Abbr.
50. Shower attention (on)
51. Zapping weapon
53. Dough dispenser
54. Comical cry
55. Coercive word on a tip jar
56. Italian or Spanish
61. Headline-making trip
62. Ran in the wash
63. Simple song
64. One who works for a queen
65. What's more

DOWN

1. Stock animal
2. Quick photo development turnaround time
3. School announcement medium
4. Tosses in a chip
5. River of Poland
6. Vessel for ashes
7. Paving material
8. Small area meas.
9. Mo. with no holidays
10. Wears the crown
11. First name of three U.S. presidents
12. The Supreme Court or a baseball team, e.g.
15. Gets all gooey?
16. French peak
18. Cabinet dept. since 1977
22. Chem. that led to some Superfund designations
23. Give up rights to
24. "Can't recall that right now"
25. White Cloud's tribespeople
28. Tackles a sub, say
29. Work on weeds
31. Aggressive personality
33. "That's finger-lickin' good!"
35. Family gal
36. Festive season
37. Like overhead bins on airplanes, often
41. Historical cooling-off periods
42. Paper size: Abbr.
43. Got warmer
44. Eight-armed mollusks
45. Conference for leaders
46. Cornball
47. Like bachelor parties
50. Art ___
52. Vacation island near Venezuela
54. Covetous feeling
55. Banjo supporter
57. Help make a play?
58. Room for experiments
59. "Act your ___!"
60. Tokyo, formerly

Reader's Choice

GAIL GRABOWSKI

46

ACROSS

1. "Funny!"
5. Life stories?
10. Censorship-fighting org.
14. Egg-shaped
15. Chick in jazz
16. Eighteenth Amendment pushers
17. *Do what can't be done
19. Castor and Olive of "Popeye"
20. Sooner ___ (at some point)
21. Less cooked, as eggs
23. Informal second-person possessive
24. Response to a bad pun
25. Go crazy (over)
28. Unflattering presentation
31. Dutch explorer Olivier van ___
32. Like some annoying voices
33. Make a play for
34. Albatross
35. Word before Island or dog
36. Painfully undecided
37. Wheelchair-bound pres.
38. They're often orange on the road
39. True alternative
40. Lighthouse alternatives
42. Wie, e.g.
43. "How to ___ Book"
44. Nerdy sort
45. Bloodred
47. Requests
51. Word before and after "against"
52. *Majority
54. Manipulates
55. Russian prince known as "Moneybag"
56. The Scarecrow's princess
57. Online crafts site
58. Source of the four starred phrases in this puzzle
59. Emulate Jesus, in the Bible's shortest verse

DOWN

1. Drifter
2. Say
3. Place for a banquet
4. Calming influences
5. Earth tones
6. Dutch South Africans
7. Old online messaging letters
8. Riot control canisterfuls
9. Shabbat, in Israel
10. God, in Hebrew
11. *Feigning an emergency
12. Singer Lovett
13. Cold War side
18. Method for testing a statistical hypothesis
22. Four-time Super Bowl–winning coach Chuck
25. Like a toggle switch
26. Putty used in auto repair
27. *Sore loser's reaction, maybe
28. Curses
29. Basketball game played by spelling its name
30. Contents of some printer cartridges
32. Alien
35. Lear daughter
36. Late-night program, say
38. Mined energy source
39. Y's in the road
41. Major religious violation
42. "You didn't hear this from me" stuff
44. "Book 'em, ___!" ("Hawaii Five-O" catchphrase)
45. Oscar nominee Elisabeth for "Leaving Las Vegas"
46. What's charged
48. Disconcert
49. "It's him ___ . . ." (relationship ultimatum)
50. Harvest
53. Allied gp. since 1948

Absolutely Fabulous

T CAMPBELL

47

ACROSS

1. Crocs' milieus
7. "Had worn them really about the ___" (line 10 of 35-Across)
11. Erstwhile transportation regulator: Abbr.
14. Food prep class
15. Pre-1917 leader
16. Cultural Revolution leader
17. Human image from line 3 of 35-Across
19. Wine bottle term
20. Parts of hearts
21. Highway charge
22. Dusting target
25. Nature image from line 1 of 35-Across
29. Should, with "to"
31. Certain letter-shaped tracks
32. Michelob alternative
34. Jai ___
35. Classic poem by 56-Across
41. Writer Leon
42. Writer Welty
43. Nancy's comics pal
46. Brewer of 32-Across
47. Time image from line 13 of 35-Across
51. Deal (out)
52. Cathedral area
53. Double Delight snacks
55. Go kaput
56. Poet whose "Early Works" are a Penguin Classic
62. Writer Nellie
63. Shuckers' units
64. Physics Nobelist ___ Isaac Rabi
65. That, to a señorita
66. Beard-busting blade
67. Monk known as "the Venerable"

DOWN

1. Alternative to Starz
2. Took the title
3. French soul
4. "Stage" in "All the world's a stage," e.g.
5. Fresh
6. Like something that gives you the willies
7. Amazing deal, slangily
8. Communication for the deaf: Abbr.
9. Fannie ___
10. Make a typo, say
11. "Don't need anymore, thanks"
12. Guitarist Santana
13. Was capable of
18. Compete
21. ___-night doubleheader
22. Outlay
23. Sexologist Westheimer
24. Mean man
26. Disney girl who adopted Stitch
27. Emulate Cicero
28. Cry from a laggard
30. However
33. Snorkel, to Beetle Bailey
34. Ques. reply
36. Gay Christian from France
37. 1949 Tracy/Hepburn film
38. NBA superstar Bryant named after a steak type
39. Word with while
40. "Great" detective of kid lit
43. Slow movers
44. Phrase from a fiancée, say
45. Western Athletic Conference player
47. "Eat, drink, ___ merry"
48. "How ___ Poem Mean?" (1975 book by John Ciardi and Miller Williams)
49. Timetable abbr.
50. Himalayan sightings
54. "The Bells ___ Mary's"
56. Actor Stephen
57. Cheerios grain
58. Cold call?
59. Work with lyrical lines
60. Lay turf
61. Half of sei

Go Your Own Way

VIC FLEMING AND BONNIE GENTRY

48

ACROSS

1. "X Games" airer
5. "Blame It on the Rain" duo ___ Vanilli
10. As a result
14. "My kingdom ___ horse!"
15. Trap at a ski lodge, say
16. Financial security
17. Photos taken at the end of a waterpark ride?
19. Memo abbr.
20. Lover of Dido, in myth
21. USN rank
23. Cookie-selling org., formerly
24. Co. in Cannes
25. Cram (together)
28. Neck of land: Abbr.
30. Judy Jetson's brother
32. The section of Paris near Notre Dame, e.g.?
35. "Our Gang" girl
37. Like many O. Henry stories
38. Sentence part: Abbr.
41. Wonderland cake words, and a hint to this puzzle's theme
43. Casino numbers game
44. "The Picture of ___ Gray"
46. All wound up
48. Military post of confusion?
50. Odist's inspiration
54. Mother ___ (kids' game)
55. "Catch-22" star Alan
57. Birth certificate info
58. K-O connection
59. Baker's no.
61. "Never Gonna Give You Up" singer Rick
63. Hippocratic ___
65. Asian river ruler?
68. Other: Sp.
69. Brings up
70. Mayberry minor
71. Florida ___ (site of the Ernest Hemingway Museum)
72. ___-Detoo of "Star Wars"
73. Exposed

DOWN

1. Wipe out
2. Cirque du ___
3. Tree surgeon, at times
4. Birth certificate info
5. "Divine" nickname in showbiz
6. First person in Frankfurt?
7. Mr. Tolstoy
8. Chinese fruit
9. Title for Jacques Clouseau: Abbr.
10. Pharmaceutical chemist Lilly
11. Cell bars?
12. "'S Wonderful" composer George
13. Prime draft status
18. School no-brainer
22. Stadium level
26. Home of the NCAA's Bruins
27. Go to pieces
29. Dracula's creator
31. Rare find
33. Deportment
34. Staff sgt., e.g.
36. Mathematician Descartes
38. Adobe file ext.
39. Dorm cohabitant
40. Knight life?
42. Unlikely to raise a ruckus
45. Within
47. Word after common or horse
49. More like a loafer
51. Slanting
52. ___ Beanie Babies
53. About 21 percent of the atmosphere
56. "You are not!" reply
58. "Check this out!"
60. Gumbo vegetable
62. Some bout results
64. Possesses
66. "The Confessions of ___ Turner"
67. Miracle-___

Have Your Cake . . .

PATRICK BLINDAUER

49

ACROSS

1. Song part that might be adjacent to a chorus
6. Joyce, namesake of a Dublin literary award
11. Tom Brady and Peyton Manning, for short
14. Whatsoever
15. 2003 Afghan film that won a Golden Globe
16. Abu Dhabi's fed.
17. "Make like a tree and leave!"
18. Wrestling Hulk
19. The Fates share one
20. "What's that movie where Simba fights Claudius on pride rock?" ("Hamlet")
22. Lay down the lawn
23. Word before history or hygiene
24. Inquisitive
26. One working on Pixar films, say
30. Grafton's "___ for Evidence"
31. Island where Homer is buried, supposedly
32. "And what's the one where Maura Tierney yells 'Out, damned spot'?" ("Macbeth")
37. ___ Lama
40. Potassium hydroxide, to chemists
41. Showing no emotion
42. "And what's the one where Amanda Bynes gets shipwrecked on Illyria?" ("Twelfth Night")
45. Fast flier
46. Faulkner's "___ Lay Dying"
47. It loses to rock
50. Seeing a movie and getting dinner, perhaps
54. Painter Paul who was a friend of Kandinsky
55. Nuke
56. "And who's the guy who directed all the books those movies were based on?"
61. Close, as a backpack

62. "Not in this lifetime, pal!"
63. Addition on the house
64. Not feeling so hot
65. Pro sports venue
66. Hawaiian veranda
67. Jargon suffix
68. Really annoying
69. Launch

DOWN

1. Huge in scope
2. Inscribe, in a way
3. One in a million
4. Zigzag skiing event
5. New York city where Mark Twain is buried
6. Philosopher whose ideas influenced the Declaration of Independence
7. "Dilbert" intern
8. Tricks at a birthday party
9. Former Obama chief of staff Rahm
10. Summer drinks made with wine and fruit
11. Mexican cheese
12. Mississippi marsh
13. Future crops
21. Feedbag filler
25. Ain't in the King's English?
26. Lends a hand
27. Biblical animal handler
28. Elba, e.g.
29. Study, bath, and kitchen
33. "Vanity Fair" author William Makepeace
34. Sensei's school
35. Malibu tourist trap
36. Play parts
38. "___ tale's best for winter"
39. "Easy as pie"
43. "Greetings!"
44. Lofgren of the E Street Band
48. Flower parts
49. Spotted around
50. Harriet's husband
51. Hammer's targets
52. Still-life fruit
53. Hangovers?

A Comedy Section of Errors

JONATHAN PORAT

1	2	3	4	5		6	7	8	9	10		11	12	13
14						15						16		
17						18						19		
20					21							22		
		23					24		25			
26	27	28				29		30					
31				32		33				34	35	36
37		38	39		40			41				
42				43			44		45			
		46			47		48	49			
50	51	52			53		54					
55			56		57				58	59	60
61		62					63			
64		65					66			
67		68					69			

57. Superman's alter ego
58. "___ Karenina"
59. Tush
60. Red sign, usually

50

ACROSS

1. Queequeg's captain
5. Giraffe relative
10. "Master and Commander" captain Aubrey
14. Cram, with "up"
15. Hooked vehicles
16. Gillette gizmo
17. Story set on actor Sean's street?
19. 1914 battle line
20. Bride, in Bari
21. Middle March?
23. Antipollution org.
24. Story about actor Oliver and his signature Mexican dish?
28. Window over a door
30. Emporium suffix
31. Away
32. Beer belly
34. More high-quality
38. Story about director Eli's vineyard?
43. "Live Free ___"
44. XLI quintupled
45. "Don't give up!"
46. Guys' counterparts
49. Paul Hogan and Russell Crowe, e.g.
52. Story about director Michael's work with lab rodents?
56. Fjord relative
57. Scrabble draw
58. Eased dress code note
61. "Last ___ to Brooklyn" (Hubert Selby, Jr. novel)
63. Story about actor Elliott's quest for the holy grail?
66. Anise-flavored liqueur
67. "___ of Two Cities"
68. Nabokov title
69. Erupt
70. Did a cobbler's job
71. "___ pin and pick it up . . ."

DOWN

1. Basics
2. Earring shape
3. Like a book with marginal writing?
4. "Soap" spin-off
5. "Catch-22" bomber pilot
6. Essential
7. International guitar month
8. Curly-haired breed
9. "It's the God's honest truth!"
10. Titular fellow in "The Great Gatsby"
11. Baffled
12. Inched
13. Fort Knox unit
18. Good listeners?
22. Neaten (up)
25. Forum wear
26. "OK, stop ringing the alarm already!"
27. Animal house
28. Baum pup
29. Essen basin
33. P.I., e.g.
35. Out of whack, on the bandstand
36. To be, overseas
37. Actor Jonathan ___ Meyers
39. Best Picture of 1958
40. Flinch, say
41. Bunch
42. Fertilization target
47. Classic cameras
48. Italian "hello!"
50. Caroled, perhaps
51. Busybodies
52. Double Stuf desserts
53. Play the matchmaker
54. Corn color
55. Himalayan nation
59. He battled Björn
60. "Giant" author Ferber
62. Haul
64. Cry upon achieving a goal?
65. Disobeyed a zoo sign, say

Steinbeck Adaptations

TONY ORBACH

51

ACROSS

1. Red dwarf, maybe
5. "Ben-Hur" studio
8. "The Birds of Pompeii" poet John who translated "The Divine Comedy"
14. UK city on the Wye
16. One of the Blues Brothers
17. Extremely anxious
18. Urban alerts
19. "The Want Bone" poet who translated "The Divine Comedy"
21. Eve of "The Vagina Monologues"
22. Like Bach's Partita No.3
23. Ad lib, musically
26. Deadly virus named for a river
29. Relinquish
30. Seeing the Serengeti, perhaps
35. Elusive children's book character
36. "Evangeline" poet who translated "The Divine Comedy"
39. Uniform color
40. U.S. soldier's three squares
41. Circle parts
42. More despicable
44. Comedy club sound
45. "THAT girl?"
46. Quebec campus
52. "Death of a Naturalist" poet who translated "The Divine Comedy"
55. Take a chance
58. "300" 300
59. Asturias's capital
60. Donkey Kong maker
61. "The Carrier of Ladders" poet W. S. who translated "The Divine Comedy"
62. "Anything else?"
63. Farmer's place, in rhyme

DOWN

1. Bilbo Baggins's home
2. Carpentry joint part
3. Some keffiyeh wearers
4. Drive away
5. 46-Across city
6. It may be covered during a tennis lesson
7. Start of the 17th century
8. Aircraft company based in Wichita
9. "___ Ike"
10. Out of whack
11. Sushi topper
12. Underworld honcho
13. Bouncers' requests
15. Cabby's client, synecdochically
20. Nonexistent
23. Molded dessert
24. Extra
25. Asks to be petted, perhaps
27. Male pal
28. Pen emanations
29. Western state, casually
30. Gershwin musical based on a Wodehouse book
31. "The Unity of India" writer Jawaharlal
32. Meal-between-meals
33. Torah holders
34. "Just so you know"
35. Fresh from the bath (and looking for a towel)
37. Test for a coll. senior, perhaps
38. Crofter's assistant
42. Pummel
43. Prepare for war
45. Johanna Spyri heroine
47. Like some checks: Abbr.
48. Like some mansions and communities
49. Puerile
50. Ivan of the court
51. Disinfectant brand
52. Twist, as data
53. Annapolis sch.
54. "Wheel of Fortune" turn
55. CD-___

A Dante-ing Task

WILL NEDIGER

56. "___ had it up to here!"
57. Newton title

52

ACROSS

1. Subject of a Bill Cosby routine that includes the line "Right! What's an ark?"
5. Fiery crime
10. Burns, e.g.
14. One on the same side
15. Volunteer's words
16. Plantation in a 1936 novel
17. Daily TV dramas (poet Alexander)
19. Language of Pakistan
20. Weapons provider
21. Loses steam?
23. Actor Torn
24. Type of suspension found in cars ("The Chronicles of Narnia" author C. S.)
27. Last Greek consonant
28. Scintilla
29. Letters that often begin an editorial on the internet
32. Pageant identifier
36. "His wife could ___ lean . . ."
38. Posthumous album by Jimi Hendrix ("The Handmaid's Tale" author Margaret)
42. Solemn toll
43. Innovative and daring
44. ___ XING (street sign)
45. Major or Minor constellation
46. Windows exit?
49. "Second star to the right, and straight on till morning" place (early science-fiction writer Jules)
56. One-time link
57. Know-it-all
58. "I'm ___ and didn't even know it!"
60. What a digital camera doesn't take
62. Former name of the tallest building in Chicago ("Uncle Tom's Cabin" author Harriet Beecher)

DOWN

1. Org. at Goddard Space Flight Center
2. Prayer starter
3. Texas Revolution battle site
4. Increase expectations
5. Nice mountain?
6. Teller of one of Chaucer's tales
7. Distribute, as flower petals
8. Native of SE Arabia
9. Homes to fly away from
10. Name that's also an alphabetic trio
11. Redheaded comedian
12. Local law
13. Brownish gray
18. Baseballs and basketballs, but not footballs
22. Avoids, with "away from"
25. It may have bullet points
26. Gravy container
29. Similar type
30. Piano solo written by Mozart
31. Inflate, as on eBay
33. Shock and ___
34. Ground cover
35. One who takes and takes
37. Gave the green light to
39. Alternative word
40. Car security feature
41. One who doesn't show his true colors?
47. Chair support
48. "In Cold Blood" author
49. Pact negotiated by Pres. Clinton
50. Like some sprays
51. "If ___ Should Leave You"
52. Some meat entrées
53. Register, as a student
54. Emphatic denial
55. Tractor pioneer John

64. Hardware fastener
65. Author Bates and singer Guthrie
66. Grocer's measure
67. Nails, as a test
68. Cotton fabric
69. "For Your ___ Only"

Inner Geniuses

TIMOTHY WESCOTT

59. "___ bien!"
61. The Rockies, briefly
63. Compass pt. opposite NNW

53

ACROSS

1. Stirred
5. Dr. Zhivago's lady
9. Taking a cruise
13. Sign at the end of a hallway, often
14. Genesis place
15. All-knowing one
16. David Caruso starring in "The Caine Mutiny"?
19. Naval Academy graduate
20. "Cocktail" that might contain pear and pineapple
22. Future docs' hurdles
24. Aquatic slitherer
25. General on Chinese restaurant menus
26. Lead-in to view or text
28. Lisbon lady
30. Wild things
32. Prepare for playing, as a piano
34. Measure of current
36. Adulterous friend?
42. Last line of defense, soccerwise
43. Inaugural event
44. Actor who loved to laugh, in "Mary Poppins"
47. Baseball defense's successes
50. Far from welcoming
51. ___ Fáil (Irish coronation stone)
52. Just barely manage
54. No longer in style
56. Military locale where orders have nothing to do with rank
59. "Slumdog Millionaire" city
62. Group laughed off stage?
64. Flaubert heroine
65. Singers Reed and Rawls
66. Sierra Club concern: Abbr.
67. Kick back
68. NCO two levels above corporal
69. Big Apple fashion initials

DOWN

1. Existed
2. Certain field animals
3. It may include hot dogs, grilled cheese, etc.
4. Set of values
5. Basic shelter
6. Sum together
7. Coral structure, say
8. Conductor Previn
9. Diva Christina with "Genie in a Bottle"
10. Edible fat
11. Raises, as a building
12. Pulitzer-winning playwright Wilson
17. "My word!"
18. Neighbor of New Brunswick
21. Neg.'s opposite
23. Slow critter
26. Concerned sch. group
27. Apply liniment, say
29. Obstetric test, for short
31. Akron, Ohio, minor leaguer
33. Provocative, as artwork
35. Poseur, in England
37. Words after "been there"
38. Northerner
39. Mellow
40. Series finale?
41. Biblical pronoun
44. Dutch ___ disease
45. Deliberate loser?
46. Message on a dirty car
48. Least racy
49. Tuxedo button
53. Things inside envelopes: Abbr.
55. Fix within
57. School terms: Abbr.
58. Some boxing decisions
60. Soon, to a poet
61. How doodles may be drawn
63. "Lemme go, ya big ___!"

Baker Street Irregulars

YAAKOV BENDAVID

53

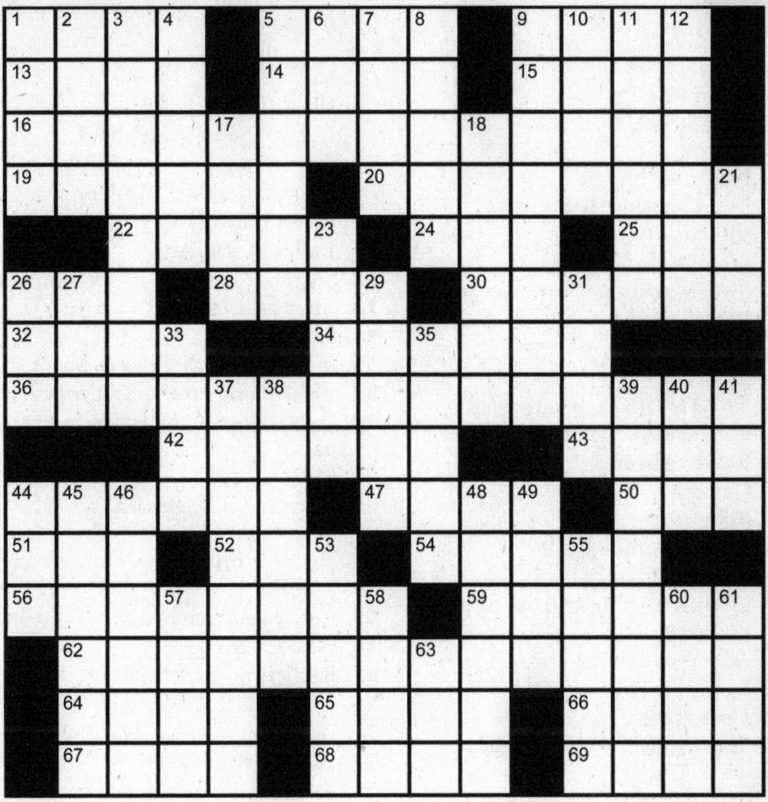

54

ACROSS

1. Eight: prefix
5. Tear into
10. Wall St. deals
14. Grad
15. Plant swelling
16. Japanese aborigine
17. Rita Mae Brown's groundbreaking novel
20. Sighting off the California coast
21. Date format
22. Hosp. staffer
23. Kemo ____
24. Novel with a sleuthing friar named Baskerville, with "The"
30. Building beams
32. Den din
33. Male or female
34. Like some taco shells
35. Fine suit material
37. Chain store founded by Ingvar Kamprad
38. Adherent's suffix
39. Really big shoe
40. Sleep spoiler
41. Classic novel about adultery, with "The"
45. One, in Berlin
46. Hawaiian tuna
47. Mambo's cousin
50. Working woman's magazine . . . and the theme of this puzzle
55. Stendhal novel subtitled "Chronique du XIXe siècle"
58. Curtain opener?
59. China's Zhou ____
60. Italian years
61. Body snatchers' flora
62. Place to get the hell out of
63. Talks a blue streak

DOWN

1. Paddles
2. Miss Peacock's game
3. Big brass
4. ____ nitrate
5. Lasso again
6. "Beats me"
7. Louvre Pyramid architect
8. Qty.
9. Domed marble mausoleum
10. NASA vehicle
11. Dallas nickname
12. Sole
13. Chop follower
18. Shoots
19. It's usually either raw or burnt
23. USAF plane for short runways
24. U.S.-Mexico-Canada commerce pact
25. Modern ___
26. "Dancing at Lughnasa" playwright Brian
27. Heroic Schindler
28. Prophet
29. It may be taken orally
30. Wife of Osiris
31. Bartlett pear alternative
35. Between 12 and 20
36. Dampens
37. Tahiti, par exemple
39. Yale for whom the university is named
40. Agatha Christie's "There Is ___"
42. Scouting missions, briefly
43. Wildlife marker
44. "Gives me ____ in the throat as deep as to the lungs . . ." (Shakespeare)
47. Many a YouTube video
48. Ulysses, for one
49. 2003 A.L. MVP
51. Sons of, Hebrew: Var.
52. Daughter of Eugene O'Neill
53. Sound at Old MacDonald's
54. Barbra's "A Star Is Born" costar
56. Brian of Roxy Music
57. "Ragtime" author's monogram

At First Blush

BRENT SVERDLOFF

55

ACROSS

1. Moved cautiously
6. ___ deux (dance for two)
11. Commercial milk source
14. Alternative to hair implants
15. Levees
16. "Come again?"
17. Memoir by Isak Dinesen
19. Baseball stat
20. Mail-order record co.
21. Be of ___ (aid)
22. Superlative suffix
23. Wine holder
25. They're detected by noses
27. Charles R. Jackson novel depicting a five-day drinking binge
33. Altar in the sky
34. Finnish architect Saarinen
35. Furniture, art, etc.
36. "Hulk" star Eric
38. Hall or Hannah
41. Movie escort, perhaps
42. Chic bathroom fixture
44. ___ chef
46. "The Heartbreak ___"
47. Robert Penn Warren novel with a title drawn from a nursery rhyme
51. Provide, as with a quality
52. Words before tear or roll
53. Deep pit member
55. Paste and epoxy
58. Babe in the woods
62. Actress Mendes
63. What the movie versions of 17-, 27-, and 47-Across won an Oscar for
65. Suffix with puppet
66. Bridge bid, briefly
67. Cliff nest
68. Pa's counterparts
69. Daniel who wrote "Flowers for Algernon"
70. Wild party

DOWN

1. Hang-gliding "Star Wars" critter
2. O.T. book after Numbers
3. Box-office take
4. Develop, in a way
5. First-rate, in old hip-hop slang
6. Some PC document files
7. Suffix with bajillion
8. Gondola alternative
9. Crack, as a secret message
10. Hockey's Tikkanen
11. Rich dessert often topped with fruit
12. Willa Cather's "One of ___"
13. Second of the five W's
18. Went for a drive
22. Teed off
24. Amber brew
26. Brit. reference
27. Woods path
28. Biker's grips
29. Mme., in Madrid
30. Some sculptures
31. Away
32. Scott in an 1857 civil rights case
33. "Mamma Mia" group
37. Big name in insurance
39. Hither's partner
40. "Dracula" made him a star
43. Seminarian's deg.
45. Frequently used ID
48. City south of Salem
49. Grammer on television
50. Where stockings may be hung
53. Overflow
54. Eye part that contains the 60-Down
56. ___ Reader
57. Long narrative poem
59. Distinctive atmosphere
60. See 54-Down
61. Places for pumps
63. ___ choy
64. Subway alternative

And the Winner Is . . .

SARAH KELLER

56

ACROSS

1. Hang in the balance
5. More with it
10. Beam with a 90-degree angle
14. Boo-boo
15. Utensil to the right of the plate, usually
16. "Say as he says, ___ shall never go" ("The Taming of the Shrew")
17. Like a stealthy thief of a magician's prop?
20. Safari highlight
21. Giving more lip
22. Noted role for Audrey
26. Snifter liquor
27. Having to sit in a very uncomfortable chair?
31. They stop at Wrigley and O'Hare
32. Canned
33. Taking practice swings, say
35. Atlantic City casino, with "The"
38. Kitty's plaint
39. Bee: Prefix
40. By way of
41. Slangy suffix with pay or plug
42. Pole position?
43. Some doubles players at Wimbledon
45. Place for a king and queen, in high school
46. Toward the rudder
48. Non-paperback OEDs?
50. Washington and Shore
53. "___ Like It"
54. Chinese soup
56. Lover
60. Adorable twins' life story, with "A"?
64. Happily-after connector
65. Actress Lindley of "Three's Company"
66. Nutritional amts.
67. Bench and Rose, for two
68. Like some business
69. Bulldogs' university

DOWN

1. ___ stick
2. Furry "Star Wars" fighter
3. Santa Maria's fleetmate
4. Place for laps, generally
5. Perform at a peak?
6. Picnic raider
7. Biomedical research org.
8. Young newts
9. Place to get clean
10. Like some diet foods, casually
11. Ideate
12. Like some grains
13. Towel off again
18. Cunning
19. California's motto
23. "Fingers crossed"
24. Opposite of nadir
25. Certain city council rep.
27. Fifteen-minute experience, according to Andy Warhol
28. Skating leap
29. Adjective for a high-tech gadget, to one baffled by it
30. Slots' arms, e.g.
34. The second Mrs. John McCain
36. Lotion additive
37. Five o'clock snarls
39. College major that may be cultural or biological, for short
44. Goat's cry
45. Fowl critters
47. DJ's controls
49. Staple for many a vegan
50. Dissuade
51. Beginnings of a donor's story
52. Until now
55. Spitting sound
57. Verdi slave girl
58. It may involve courses
59. Latin 101 verb
61. Dict. entries
62. TV planet
63. Coral isle

Shifty Eyes

DANIEL A. FINAN

57

ACROSS

1. Convene
5. Wowed sounds
8. Site of Nigel Davies' ancient kingdoms
12. Country album?
14. Alternative to Guesses
16. Pungent emanation
17. Jazz singer with "New Moon Daughter"
20. Hooded sweatshirt part
21. Oil source, perhaps
22. 1948 Hitchcock film
24. Don Quixote cardinal
25. Glass of "This American Life"
28. Junk bond rating
31. Carla Tortelli portrayer on "Cheers"
34. High-pressure pitch?
36. Native Alaskan people
37. Royal Geographical Society journal
38. Jane, who played Spock's mother
41. Greek seduced by a feathery Zeus
42. Baba Yaga, for one
44. Defenseless village's scourge
46. Former White House Press Corps stalwart
49. Word after common or golden
50. Senate vote
51. Greek P
52. Short golf stroke
54. Julia Child dessert
56. Stevenson's doctor's alter ego
60. "Jamaica Inn" author
64. Verdi opera commissioned by an Egyptian Khedive
65. St.-John's-___
66. Runs afoul of the International Olympic Committee
67. Muffin ingredient
68. Obama's domain ending
69. "Venerable" English saint

DOWN

1. Glaswegian coats
2. Catchall abbr.
3. Besides
4. Police weapon with a "drive stun" mode
5. Like the lady who swallowed a fly
6. Perseus or Hercules
7. Close hermetically
8. "The Worst Journey in the World" destination
9. People people: Abbr.
10. Christopher Robin's hoppy friend
11. Keats's object of contemplation
13. Enjoys every bite
15. Pen dwellers
18. One's kid's cousin
19. Piano key material, once
23. Hard to get your hands on
25. Get in the way of
26. Bay Area athlete
27. Turkish capital
28. Cuban dance
29. "The Truman Show" actor Jim
30. Southern culinary style
32. Dollar alternative
33. Doozy
35. Hans Christian Andersen, e.g.
39. Compress, as espresso
40. Psychological shock
43. Where "The Smartest Guys in the Room" worked
45. Bossa nova artist Gilberto
47. Completely confused
48. Sodium-rich meat treat
53. Pulsate
54. "Truth is more of a stranger ___ fiction" (Mark Twain)
55. Greek coin
57. "Golly jeepers!"
58. Title document
59. Gaelic language
60. Smidgen
61. Put on the schedule
62. Palm product
63. Former "TRL" airer

Greek Sorority

ANNE BRETHAUER

58

ACROSS

1. Security system feature
6. State secrets?
10. Galahad and Lancelot, e.g.
14. "Is it too risky for me?"
15. Get ready for the national anthem
16. Over again
17. Starts admitting customers
18. Synagogue cabinets
19. "Would ___ to you?"
20. T. S. Eliot: "Whither Trash"?
23. WWII assault vessel
26. "What a piece of work is ___" ("Hamlet")
27. Look around online
28. Main arteries
30. How some learn music
32. Sinclair Lewis: "Running Through Town"?
34. Patriotic org. of which Laura Bush is a member
37. Too many cooks might spoil it
38. Bol. neighbor
39. Sporty '80s Pontiac
41. Sizzling sound
42. Edgar Allan Poe: "Forty-niner's Fever"?
44. Take by force
46. Gather, with "up"
47. Catches sight of
50. Informal greetings
51. Game, ___, match
52. William Shakespeare: "Evening for an Epiphany"?
56. Bunker, for one
57. Thief's take
58. "Shucks!"
62. Sweet sandwich-type cookie
63. HS reunion attendee
64. Robe fabric
65. Whole lot
66. Not a boon
67. Songwriter Gainsbourg

DOWN

1. Commotion
2. Once around a track
3. "You ___ here"
4. Check for a flat?
5. Hodgepodge
6. Muscleman's quality
7. Old Italian currency
8. Seeks permission
9. Least risky option
10. One at the helm
11. Oft-ridiculed relative
12. Guides for steeds
13. The founder of IKEA, e.g.
21. Virginia, relative to West Virginia
22. Big name in laundry detergent
23. Young bleaters
24. Skyrockets
25. Small musical groups
29. Rubble maker
30. Soft headgear
31. Vault cracker
33. Cheers from a crowd
34. Collection agency concerns
35. As ___ (in most cases)
36. Name synonymous with synonyms
39. Some annual injections
40. Reading material for border guards?
42. Research site
43. Not a repro: Abbr.
44. "Weeping" tree
45. NBA arbiter
47. Spirit of the people
48. Emulate an eddy
49. Martinique volcano
50. Blackjack command
53. Spanish greeting
54. It may be proper
55. The old you?
59. [My owner said not to let anyone through here!]
60. Work unit
61. Watch closely

Subtitles

GAIL GRABOWSKI AND ED KROLAK

58

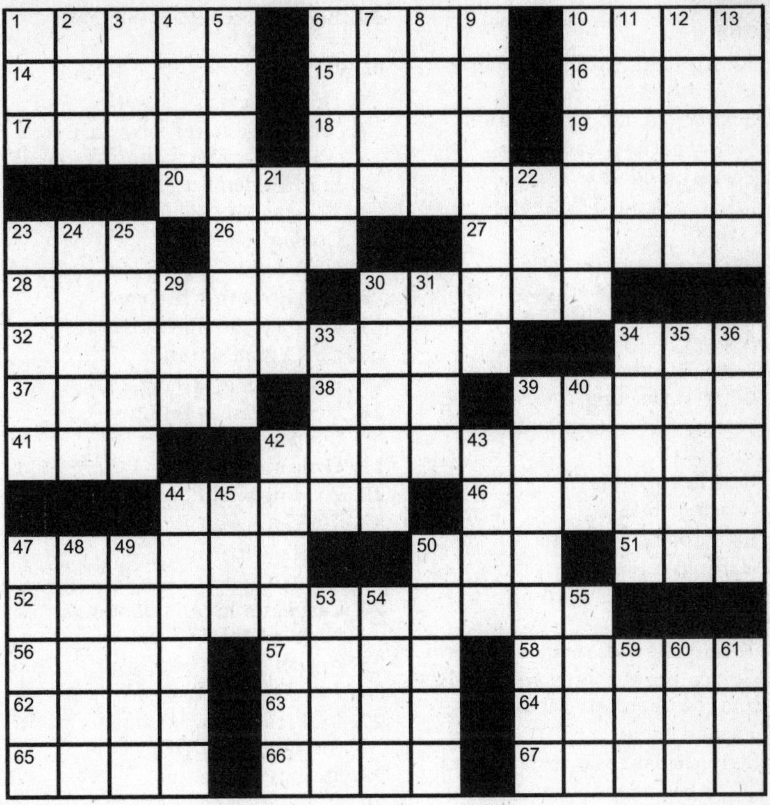

59

ACROSS

1. Family name in "The Grapes of Wrath"
5. Small circulation publication
9. Pointy pottery fragment
14. Pervasive quality
15. School attended by George Orwell
16. Bet
17. Misanthropic poet in Thomas Love Peacock's "Nightmare Abbey"
19. Clear, as a chalkboard
20. Cigarette leaving
21. Setting for "Antony and Cleopatra"
22. Bunches of birds
23. Fencing blades
25. Inventor's protections
26. Darlings
28. Pink and frilly, in juvenile stereotypes
29. "Golden Boy" dramatist Clifford
30. Golden ticket source, in "Charlie and the Chocolate Factory"
33. Thick volume
34. Stringed Japanese instruments
35. "___ a beauteous evening, calm and free" (Wordsworth)
37. Polyctor, e.g., in "The Iliad"
39. Bit of evidence
40. Country near Bahrain
41. University of Arizona city
42. Progress, in fitness equipment ads
45. Elie Wiesel memoir
46. Something or someone
47. Type type
48. ___ Grande
51. Observe Yom Kippur, e.g.
52. Fighting rabbit in "Watership Down"
54. Plastic clogs brand
55. Pain
56. Just fine
57. Native American dwelling
58. Bambi, for one
59. Boomers' children, for short

DOWN

1. Dr.'s magazine
2. "You will answer 'The slaves are ___'" ("The Merchant of Venice")
3. Lord Voldemort, to Harry Potter
4. "One ___ in the Life of Ivan Denisovich"
5. Nobodies
6. Gossip column listings
7. Cyrano's prominent feature
8. USNA grad's rank
9. How the sirens sang, in myth
10. Hero of James Fenimore Cooper's "The Spy"
11. Once more
12. Bowling alley button
13. Put clothes on
18. Hunts, with "on"
22. Minstrel poets
24. Carpenter in "A Midsummer Night's Dream"
25. Attach, as a corsage
26. Attractive, so to speak
27. Basketball player Lamar (Anagram: MOOD)
28. Swamp reptile
30. Concluding musical sections
31. In one action
32. Puerto ___
34. Purrer
36. One of 100 in D.C.
38. Hammett's "The ___ Falcon"
39. Gently pull on
41. Heart, slangily
42. Show one's emotions
43. ___ nous
44. Place to sit, in front of a brownstone
45. Ecological role
47. Deep purple
49. Setting for the graphic novel and film "Persepolis"

Tree People

RAY HAMEL

50. Clock material in "Cannery Row"

52. "Then she told me all about the ___place, and I said I wished I was there" (Huck Finn)

53. Harley-Davidson, casually

60

ACROSS

1. Three or four, say
5. "Profiles in Courage" author, initially
8. Jacuzzi, e.g.
14. Effectuate
15. ASUS ___ PC 1000HE
16. Revisions, of a sort
17. John Donne's former job
19. Herman Melville's former job
20. Stupid and ill-mannered
22. "Oh, clever!"
23. Printer's selection
26. Lew Wallace's former job
29. Thomas Hardy's former job
33. "Watchmen" author Moore
34. Busting org.
35. Not well
36. Hendrix hairstyle, briefly
37. Lewis Carroll's former job
43. Boat propeller
44. Author McEwan
45. Take a bough?
47. Application for windows?
49. O. Henry's former "job"
52. John Keats's former job
54. Honeymoon locale, perhaps
55. Gardner once married to Sinatra
56. Composer of the opera "William Tell"
60. Langston Hughes's former job
63. Honoré de Balzac's former job
67. "Fighting" collegiate team
68. Soirée invitee
69. Curriculum range
70. From Florence, e.g.
71. Shakespeare contemporary Jonson
72. Depot posting, for short

DOWN

1. Rock tool?
2. Not in range, say
3. Barely manage, with "out"
4. Riches
5. Ancient king of Israel
6. Measures in prosody
7. Actress Russell
8. Pronoun with a slash
9. Miner's material
10. ___-la-la (singsong syllables)
11. Socialite Beckwith
12. Resident of 24-Down, e.g.
13. Everyday
18. Sandwich shop chain
21. Certain NCO
23. Rage
24. Beehive State city
25. Org. with a 64-team tournament
27. 34-Across employee
28. Weena's fictional race
30. Wedding cake layer
31. "Slippery" tree
32. Insurance issuance
36. Punishment for a minor infraction
38. Asian secret society
39. Despise
40. A generous person might pick it up
41. Penne ___ vodka
42. December song
46. Butt in
47. Least populous UN member
48. Train tracks shaped like letters
49. Ambient composer Brian
50. Penny metal
51. Ten-point draws in Scrabble
52. Certain negative response to "should we rent this movie?"
53. Senator Hatch
57. Concrete piece
58. Undifferentiated
59. Champion's cry
61. Quirk
62. Bambi's aunt
64. Lodge member
65. Letters above 0-0-0, before the baseball game starts
66. Little butter?

Moonlighting

BRENDAN EMMETT QUIGLEY

61

ACROSS

1. Credit card balance, e.g.
5. Express skepticism
10. Meal cooked in a large pot, perhaps
14. "Pinocchio" goldfish
15. Baseball fielder's flub
16. Modern Siamese
17. Kindergarten sculptor's medium
18. Obsolete TV attachments
20. Word before mass or mattress
21. Attic corner sights
22. The "J" of J. K. Rowling
23. Laments
25. Move like the Road Runner
26. Basilica area
27. All that one can stand
31. Comic page feature
33. Looks seriously afraid
34. "Dear Yoko" honoree
35. Tackle a trail
36. Novelist's stock-in-trade
37. Graph's x or y
38. "___ never been so insulted!"
39. Biblical land with a queen
40. Painted Desert structure
41. Critical remarks
43. Offensive to Miss Manners
44. Involuntary twitches
45. "___ allowed!" (exclusionary sign in some boys' clubhouses)
48. 1994 skating medalist Baiul
51. Promises to pay
52. Laboratory animal
53. Joel Chandler Harris narrator
55. Senator's gofer
56. Durable Asian wood
57. Sponge out
58. He scored 1,281 soccer goals
59. Prepares, as a trap
60. Some brasses, briefly
61. "Title" for the 53-Across characters that begin 18-Across and 3- and 28-Down

DOWN

1. 1983 Mr. T movie
2. "Dallas" matriarch
3. Wall Street condition, at times
4. Play thing
5. Tranquil
6. Chronic complainers
7. Moons, planets, et al.
8. Watch pocket
9. Beans, in Mexican cuisine
10. Like many romance novels
11. By comparison to
12. Garner through effort
13. Herriot's "All Things ___ and Wonderful"
19. Handyman's helpers
21. Six-legged nest builder
24. Early role for Ronny Howard
25. Princess in many Nintendo games
27. Comments at a roast
28. Short dog breed with an erect tail
29. Military division
30. Suffer defeat
31. Melville's Pequod, e.g.
32. VCR successor
33. They do lines for a living
36. "So what?"
37. Volkswagen subsidiary
39. Excel
40. Ticks, or ticks off
42. Follows stealthily
43. Stirs from sleep
45. Pointless
46. Soup dispenser
47. Handle the handlebars of
48. Tattles on
49. Joint below the femur
50. Jazz improv singing style
51. Film format for domed theaters
54. Geological period
55. SFPD alert

Relatively Speaking

PATRICK JORDAN

62

ACROSS

1. Interstices
5. Milne marsupial
10. Potter's need
14. Staple character in a Pearl Buck novel
15. Big name in computer chips
16. Garden sprayer
17. Optimistic
18. Prescribed amounts
19. Butterfinger's exclamation
20. Rejected classic #1: Mann's bio of athlete Zola and filmmaker Mel
23. Maker of frozen spuds
24. Borscht necessity
27. Quintessence
32. Chou En-___
33. Cuernavaca coins
37. Rejected classic #2: Melville's bio of a brooding bloodsucker
39. Question to Brutus
40. Snorer's breathing problem, perhaps
41. Mayberry moppet
42. Rejected classic #3: Brontë's bio of a shackle fortune legatee
44. Higher learning spots: Abbr.
45. One may be rolled or steel-cut
46. Containers for the Tin Man
48. Contemptuous look
50. Posthumously published work by Mario Puzo
55. Rejected classic #4: Shelley's bio of diarist Anne and writer Gertrude
60. Get a price for, in the checkout lane
62. "The Color Purple" heroine
63. Bevy of bovines
64. Former Cunard flagship, briefly
65. Gladiator's milieu
66. At any time
67. Still feeling the workout, say
68. "You've been ___ lifesaver!"
69. ___-majesté

DOWN

1. Greta of old Hollywood
2. Subject of many chansons
3. ___ deux (type of dance)
4. 1981 media epithet for Prince Charles's blushing bride-to-be
5. Take, often for ransom
6. Give ___ to (approve of)
7. Air disaster investigation agcy.
8. Actor Will, of "The Waltons"
9. Too
10. Crack under pressure
11. They sink ships, supposedly
12. Killer in "Antony and Cleopatra"
13. Agreeable response
21. Sweet summer coolers
22. Controversial marriage vow verb
25. Unspoken
26. "Oliver Twist" villain Bill
28. Urge forward
29. Quinine-flavored beverage
30. Wagnerian production
31. ___ culpa
33. Rio Grande feeder
34. Wharton's Frome
35. Place for ribs and ribbons
36. Avignon assent
38. Heavy unit
40. Sashimi fish
43. "A Doll's House" heroine
44. Doctrines
47. Possible response on a Howie Mandel game show
49. Bert's roommate
51. Lucy's gal pal
52. Teller of the third Canterbury tale
53. Set on the road
54. ___ 3000 (OutKast member)
56. Frozen Four org.
57. Brynner's "The King and I" costar
58. Out of the wind
59. Columbian vessel
60. Trafalgar and Red: Abbr.
61. Corp. honcho

Shot Out of the Canon

DONNA LEVIN

63

ACROSS

1. Mensa admission criteria
4. Episode in a long-running serial
10. With 69-Across, author who theorized 39-Across
14. ___ generis (unique)
15. Athenian magistrate
16. Hip bones
17. Soup pot top
18. "A date which will live in infamy" site
20. "Before ___ you go . . ."
22. At an end
23. Normal: Abbr.
24. Sheetrock or drywall, to some
29. Prefix with postale
30. "The ___ something big"
34. Turned off by
38. Coin introduced on 1/1/99
39. "Capital" idea, and a feature of each theme entry
43. Confident mantra
44. Awaiting trial, say
45. World-famous cubist
49. Viennese article
50. Like an egotist
55. Orienteering tool: Abbr.
58. Beams of light
59. Without a partner
60. One who matures more slowly
65. Little genius?
66. Mil. fliers
67. Appoint to the clergy
68. Frequent title starter
69. See 10-Across
70. Gorgon with snakes for hair
71. Notre, as in Notre Dame

DOWN

1. Long Island community
2. Hedgehog pricker
3. Hit single, perhaps, on a 45
4. Tommyrot
5. Is, for many
6. "His Master's Voice" brand
7. Pulsate
8. Some Swedish cars
9. Ready to mate, as a cat
10. White wine and cassis aperitif
11. Priestly vestments
12. Mob activity?
13. Piecrust ingredient
19. 2009 stimulus package, officially: Abbr.
21. Anastasia and Alexandra, e.g.
25. Trueheart of "Dick Tracy"
26. ". . . ___ saw Elba"
27. Commercial prefix with Rooter
28. Idealists, to some
31. Big brass
32. "Straight up ___ the rocks?"
33. Henry or Harrison
34. Take ___ (swim)
35. Third word of Caesar's boast
36. Remove from the scene, briefly
37. Lennon's partner
40. First-floor apartment
41. Final weekdays: Abbr.
42. Conan O'Brien predecessor
46. Certain Slav
47. Downhill event
48. Long past
51. "Does it strike you ___ that . . ."
52. Show respect for, as a queen
53. Yale's namesake
54. Earthmover, for short
55. Sorrowful
56. "¿Qué ___?"
57. Film critic's unit
61. Special ___ (film production abbr.)
62. Former Kenyan guerrillas, when doubled
63. Winter woe in Wiesbaden
64. Genetic letters

Kapital Letters

LEONARD WILLIAMS

64

ACROSS

1. With 73-Across, what the clue for 17-, 41-, or 65-Across is, relative to its answer
6. Gain web access
11. Sea rescue letters
14. Item on a to-do list
15. Last Oldsmobile model made
16. QB's try
17. *Paul French
19. Broadway's Hagen
20. Item on an iPod
21. Prefix with thermal
22. Become perfect at
24. Supervise
27. Side benefit of a job
28. World's third-largest island
31. Mollycoddle, with "on"
33. "Honest" prez
34. Pisa dough
37. "Well, ___ darned!"
41. *Anson MacDonald
44. Street mentioned in "Walking in Memphis"
45. Actor Nick of "North Dallas Forty"
46. Mercury or Mars, but not Earth
47. "___ Anything for Love" (Meatloaf single)
49. Try to get a better price
51. War-loving Olympian
54. Tangle up
57. Deprived
59. NRC predecessor
60. Early Platte River dwellers
64. Tenn. neighbor
65. *Leonard Spaulding
68. Profs' aides
69. Triangular road sign
70. Worn (away)
71. Photographer's asset
72. Cary of "The Princess Bride"
73. See 1-Across

DOWN

1. CBS military series
2. Extremely
3. Sound of pleasure or pain
4. Fire-breathing creature of myth
5. Common Market initials
6. One nearly cut James Bond in half in "Goldfinger"
7. Goulashes
8. Precious stone
9. Start of Juliet's lament
10. PBS science series
11. Pan-fry
12. Bewhiskered river critter
13. Desolate
18. Lose eligibility because of being too old
23. Put letters together
25. Swerved
26. Finned '50s flop
28. Nasty remark
29. An orchestra may tune to one
30. Grammy-winning singer McEntire
32. Musical ineptitude
35. Talked and talked
36. "Well, looky here!"
38. ___ Mason (investment firm)
39. Life sci.
40. Conclusion: Ger.
42. Beethoven dedicatee
43. Cornell University city
48. Bit of fine print
50. Related to the whole planet
51. Diminish
52. Race that's run collaboratively
53. Delete, as files
55. Expensive fur source
56. Revenge seekers, in a series of teen films
58. Actress Soleil Moon ___
61. Ballet attire
62. Central Utah city
63. Last word of a New Year's Eve tune
66. Bow wood
67. Barney Fife's position: Abbr.

Space Aliases

PANCHO HARRISON

65

ACROSS

1. Do some elementary math
4. "Kill Bill" actress Thurman
7. Suffix for a philosophy
10. Source of some monthly stress: Abbr.
13. Mariner
14. Something you might kick down the road
15. Co. with ads featuring Nipper, once
16. Indian novelist Santha Rama ___
17. McCarthy novel about a father who "hadn't kept a calendar for years"
19. Trying
21. Part of the acronym ALF
22. Words in a Doris Day song title
23. Ellison classic about a loner who "people refuse to see"
27. Check quickly
30. "Who ___ to say?"
31. But, to Brutus
32. Cyclades Island
33. Rod Stewart's ex
35. They may represent programs
39. Seuss book about a character who "would not, could not, in a box"
42. Hilton rival
43. Skip the ceremony, in a way
44. "The Stand" protagonist
45. Upton Sinclair novel adapted into the film "There Will Be Blood"
47. Acute visitation locales, for short
48. Slang exclamation that was Merriam-Webster's Word of the Year in 2007
49. Shelley novel about a creature that was "fearless, and therefore powerful"
54. Make sure every last bit of dirt is off, say
55. Sasha or Malia
59. Totally chilled out?
60. Like the characters referenced in 17-, 23-, 39-, and 49-Across
62. Pilot's approximation: Abbr.
63. El ___ (Warrior from Castile)
64. 3-D hosp. picture
65. Dispensable candy featured in a "Seinfeld" episode
66. Mexican couple?
67. Hawaii's Mauna ___
68. Source of some D.C. funding
69. Part of many Quebec place names

DOWN

1. "___ girl!"
2. Roald who created Mr. Fox and Willy Wonka
3. Zwei follower
4. Big East school, familiarly
5. Kid's cry?
6. "What else?"
7. Novelist Fouad al-Tikerly, e.g.
8. Surgeon's garb
9. Baked good associated with Marcel Proust
10. Literary introduction
11. "NewsRadio" actress Tierney
12. Sontag with the essay "Notes on 'Camp'"
18. Horse halter
20. Cheap musical purchase, nowadays
24. Low-lying region
25. Reputation
26. Some cruisegoers
27. [At least I tried . . .]
28. "Boy Meets World" boy
29. Away from port
33. Agent that increases fuel octane rating
34. Of ___ (somewhat)
36. Very, very
37. Defense gp. headquartered in Brussels
38. Lewd material
40. Athletic shoe brand
41. Basilica of St. Francis of Assisi section

Whaddayacallem

BEAU STING

46. Lisa who was the first person to dunk in the 48-Down

48. League for 46-Down

49. Cooked, as onion rings

50. Page facing a verso

51. Fields of expertise

52. Canio's wife in "Pagliacci"

53. Neither Doric nor Corinthian

56. They're switched off for an unplugged set

57. Greet partner

58. Woodworking blade

60. Loudest voice in the ballpark, often

61. Powerful lobbying gp.

66

ACROSS

1. Animation frame
4. Lady's partner, in animation, with "The"
9. "The Divine ___"
14. Duct opening?
15. Prefix meaning "sun"
16. Madcap
17. '90s General Motors brand
18. Second president of Turkey
19. Certain Zoroastrian
20. With 27-Across, how Launcelot says he'll take leave of Shylock in Act II
23. Russian cosmonaut Gherman
24. Long-range Reagan era program, for short
25. Option for getting online
27. See 20-Across
30. BLT part
33. Word after any of the five W's
36. Noble title
37. Jessica's comment on romance in Act II
41. "Norma" or "Fidelio"
43. Indian garment for women
44. Rue
46. See 8-Down
52. Producer Brian
53. Lubricate
56. Keep an ___ the ground
57. See 54-Down
62. Declaration for one unafraid of a raise
63. More than simmering
64. Irritate
65. Cowardly Lion's acquisition
66. Exuberance
67. Hillary Clinton, ___ Rodham
68. "Danse Macabre" composer Camille Saint-___
69. Fictional evangelist Gantry
70. All-powerful figure

DOWN

1. Beginning of a Cartesian statement
2. Regardless of whether
3. Ray of "GoodFellas"
4. Steal
5. Flat rate?
6. "That's ___ blow" ("Shame on you for doing that!")
7. Short skirts
8. With 46-Across, what Shylock sues to collect in Act IV
9. Frequent delivery
10. Letters on the cross, in some paintings
11. Run-of-the-mill
12. Serenades
13. Former telecom industry letters
21. Darlin'
22. First-aid ___
26. Actor Chaney
28. Start of a hoedown shout
29. They matriculate in New Haven
31. ___-Wan Kenobi
32. Fellow
34. Fed. agcy.
35. Major river of Spain
37. Summer stand drink
38. Slag source
39. Delivery vehicle
40. Mr. ___ (Boston rapper)
41. Bullfight cry
42. Universal remedy
45. New walker, perhaps
47. Tentative proposal
48. Baseball's Angels, on the scoreboard
49. Dr. J's last name
50. Less than quadraphonic
51. Emulated a goose
54. With 57-Across, ironic court cry of Shylock during Act IV
55. Media lawyer's concern
58. ___ Mills Portrait Studios
59. "___ Well That Ends Well"
60. "Cheers" regular
61. Honeybee's home
62. Contacts, in a way, online

The Merchant's Tale

VIC FLEMING AND BONNIE GENTRY

(crossword grid puzzle, numbered 1–70)

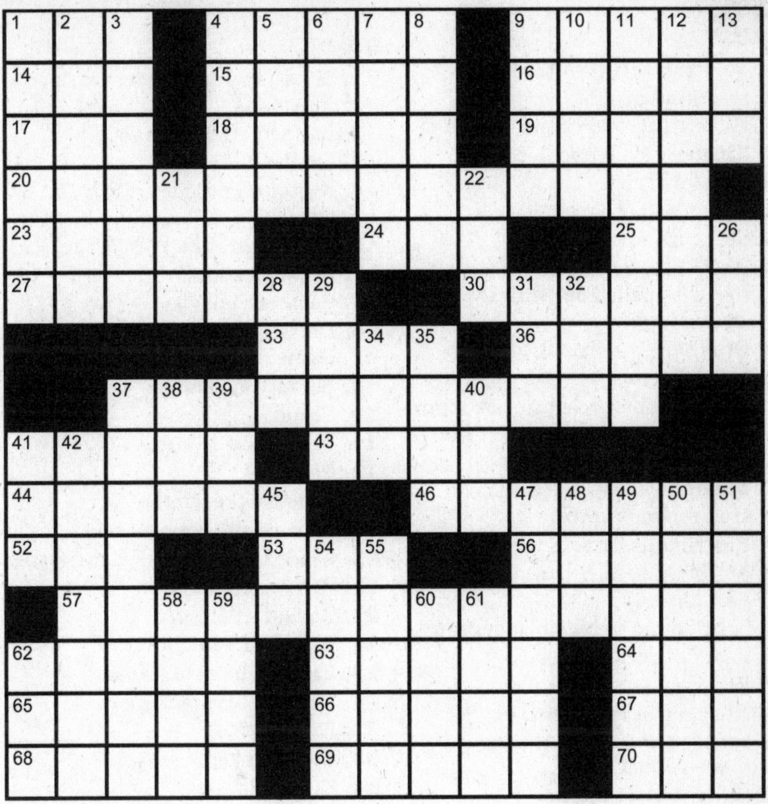

67

ACROSS

1. ___ Panisse (Alice Waters restaurant)
5. Hit with an open hand
9. Japanese soup noodle
13. Taj Mahal city
14. Zeus's better half
15. Silent film star Naldi
16. Radio play by the author whose name is spelled out with the circled letters
19. Deckhand's affirmation
20. Talmudic tongue
22. Novel by the circled author about a rich guy who pays to save his own life
27. "Alas and alack!"
28. History book verb
29. Roadside assistance gp.
30. Macbeth, before Duncan's murder
32. "The Sound of Music" mountains
34. Keats's Grecian object
35. Retainer or toll
36. Early novel by the circled author also known as "The Shipwrecked"
41. Golfer's little helper
42. Sloth or gluttony
43. Denim pioneer Strauss
45. 17-Down, for example, when heated
48. Brand for "choosy moms"
49. Conference for LSU and Ole Miss
50. "___ boom bah!"
51. Novel by the circled author adapted into an Alan Ladd film
56. Acid neutralizers
58. "___ of Love" (Pacino film)
59. Novel by the circled author adapted into a Julianne Moore film, with "The"
65. Brown, when describing horses
66. "Just a little bruise, that's all"
67. Eggshell color cousin

DOWN

1. Musician Yusuf Islam's former nickname
2. Banned MLB substance
3. Shelley's "before"
4. Restaurant guide creator Tim or Nina
5. Martin on "The West Wing"
6. Rural meadow
7. Curator's purview
8. Doris Day musical "The ___ Game"
9. Like spam, usually
10. Carpe ___
11. Where the Senators skate
12. Country
17. "The Catcher in the ___"
18. Man-mouse connection
21. Grade that just makes the grade
22. Pan Am competitor
23. Robust
24. "Baseball Tonight" airer
25. Lake in the mountains
26. Submits for grading
31. Foot part
33. York and Pepper, e.g.
34. Dubai's locale
35. "We're #1!" shouter
37. "Not to mention . . ."
38. Vex
39. Suburb of Phoenix
40. Daredevil Knievel
44. Jack Daniel's rocks
45. Taker of liquids at the airport
46. Former Houston NFL team
47. Beginning of a famous JFK appeal
48. Pop musician Timberlake
52. JPG alternative
53. Major Japanese port
54. Striped judiciary
55. More padded, perhaps
57. Forever's partner
60. Blue Cross Blue Shield service

68. Eyelid issue
69. Sext- plus three
70. Catch a few winks

In His Own Words

NATHAN MILLER

61. Untold years
62. Pitcher at the top of the rotation
63. Org. concerned with W-2s
64. Slump

68

ACROSS

1. Airport guesses
5. Like "m" and "n" sounds
10. Resistance units
14. Smallest member of the litter
15. Chilled, as champagne
16. Capital of Italia
17. Made less serious
19. In the thick of
20. "Father and Son" was written by Edmund Gosse, while "Fathers and Sons" was written by ___
22. Demolished a building, in Dorchester
24. Alban who was a contemporary of Schoenberg
25. Type of nontoxic dye
26. "Four and twenty blackbirds baked in ___ . . ."
30. Michelle of "Crouching Tiger, Hidden Dragon"
33. "Martin Chuzzlewit" was written by Charles Dickens, while "Martin Eden" was written by ___
37. Ivan the Terrible, e.g.: Var.
39. Et ___ (and others, in Latin)
40. Greek alphabet ender
41. See 54-Down
42. Chief
43. "The Golden Bough" was written by Sir James Frazer, while "The Golden Bowl" was written by ___
45. As well
47. Former Zairian president Mobutu ___ Seko
48. Denom. founded in Philadelphia
49. Police employee: Abbr.
52. Dadaist Max
54. "The Secret Garden" was written by Frances Hodgson Burnett, while "The Secret Agent" was written by ___
59. Animator Disney
60. Hovercraft's inflatable base
63. "Bus Stop" playwright William
64. Flat and gray
65. River to the Rhine, in Germany
66. Ten-speed component
67. Written reminders
68. Aspiring lawyer's test

DOWN

1. Before, to Robert Burns
2. Wedding rental
3. Unlikely to mix and mingle
4. Comic actor Carell
5. Mad Libs category
6. Med. student's study
7. In ___ (in original position)
8. Sharp-tasting
9. Shelf
10. Hot, citrusy brew
11. Heart locale?
12. Year for Super Bowl XXXVIII
13. Down in the dumps
18. Tennis star Rafael
21. Mock ending?
22. Prince from India
23. Rhododendron relative
27. Hundred Acre Wood bear
28. "She Believes ___" (1978 Kenny Rogers song)
29. Paradisiac places
31. Shelley sonnet about "a traveler from an antique land"
32. Charmers' female entourages, slangily
34. Younger sibling, perhaps
35. Fairy tale antagonist
36. House votes
38. Put back to 00:00, say
44. Greets the visiting team, perhaps
46. Prime number divisor
50. Muscle twitch
51. Suffix for lovers?
53. 1986 Indianapolis 500 winner Bobby
54. With 41-Across, a Brontë protagonist
55. Olympic gymnast Korbut
56. Study at the last minute
57. Tetra- times two
58. Van ___, California

How Close Are They?

MATT JONES

1	2	3	4		5	6	7	8	9		10	11	12	13
14					15						16			
17				18							19			
		20								21				
22	23							24						
25				26	27	28	29			30		31	32	
33			34				35	36		37				38
39				40						41				
42				43				44						
	45			46		47					48			
		49		50	51				52	53				
	54	55				56	57	58						
59				60								61	62	
63				64						65				
66				67						68				

59. Top portion of some Halloween costumes

61. ___ pro nobis

62. Badminton divider

69

ACROSS

1. Okinawa's country
6. Valuable thing to have
11. Hemingway moniker
15. "Numb3rs" character Ramanujan
16. Till the soil once more
17. Baldwin of "30 Rock"
18. Hawaiian crooner
19. "I Still See ___" ("Paint Your Wagon" song)
20. Poet Ogden on a 2002 U.S. postage stamp
21. *Deer, dove
24. Deep-voiced singer Simone
25. "NYPD Blue" star Morales
26. Commercial pet
29. Set of values
32. Venerate
36. Figure skating jump
37. Primary strategy
38. Algonquian language
39. Henri's honey
40. Defiles
42. Designer Saint Laurent
43. Not from the States
45. Man of ___ (Superman sobriquet)
46. Wise one
47. Get the picture
48. Tyler of "Ghost Whisperer"
49. ___ Bator
50. Big pile
52. Repair shop guesses: Abbr.
54. *Peacock, grains, caduceus
62. Pleased
63. Vigilant
64. "Little ___" (small East Coast state nickname)
65. Buster Brown's bulldog
66. Russian breakfast option
67. Nail polish ingredient
68. Peace symbol shapes
69. Simplest Roman sandal
70. Eastwood's "Rawhide" role

DOWN

1. Will Smith's wife
2. Bow-wielding boy of paintings
3. Canning jar size
4. *Aegis, thunderbolt, invisibility helmet
5. Author Wolf
6. *Vulture, globe, lyre
7. Ward who played Teddy on "Sisters"
8. Transport commercially
9. *Dawn, witches, hearth
10. They're shed while bawling
11. *Flocks, wine, lions
12. Jai ___ (fast-paced sport)
13. Gadfly
14. Post-exercise pain
22. Not competent
23. Pearl Harbor locale
26. Loud noise
27. Sense of ___
28. 1986 autobiography
30. Neighbor of the Dominican Republic
31. Actress Laura of "ER"
33. Maritime
34. Swiss luxury watch
35. Up and about
41. Dividing mark
44. Project info, for short
51. Basra natives, e.g.
53. Towel material
54. "Design on a Dime" network
55. Saab or Tahari of fashion
56. Mania
57. Armstrong of Apollo 11
58. Large Parisian vase
59. Pretty much all
60. Falco of "The Sopranos"
61. Roget's wds.

Heavenly Symbols

VIVIAN COLLINS

1	2	3	4	5		6	7	8	9	10		11	12	13	14
15						16						17			
18						19						20			
21					22						23				
			24						25						
26	27	28			29		30	31			32		33	34	35
36					37						38				
39					40				41		42				
43				44		45					46				
47						48					49				
			50		51				52		53				
54	55	56				57	58					59	60	61
62					63						64				
65					66						67				
68					69						70				

70

ACROSS

1. 451, at the Forum
5. Breakfast strips
10. Actress Jessica
14. Focus (in on)
15. Like Humpty Dumpty
16. Female who, at least, has her pride?
17. Jordanian, e.g.
18. Two-time Oscar winner Davis
19. Vulcan mind ___
20. In 1938, one was real news to people who tuned in late
23. Take advantage of Black Friday
24. Put on solid food
25. Reaction triggered by a certain 20-Across
33. "Yoo-___!"
34. Relative of -ance
35. Milan's La ___ opera house
36. Hydrocarbon endings
38. What the 20-Across was based on
41. Arias, e.g.
42. Turkish currency
44. Trompe l' ___ (optical trickery)
46. Dugout boss: Abbr.
47. Event that began in Grover's Mill, in the 20-Across
51. Bit of poop?
52. Star quality, sometimes
53. With "The," 38-Across that inspired the 20-Across
60. Kachina carver
61. Related on the mother's side
62. Chess castle
63. Test that may be "popped"
64. Reef life
65. Like flan
66. ___-ball (arcade game)
67. Fabric with a diagonal weave
68. Drop, as pounds

DOWN

1. Drug ___ (informal title coined by Joe Biden in 1982)
2. Explorer of children's TV
3. Fill a .44, say
4. Toss back
5. Updo doohickey
6. State flatly
7. Roman namesake of a libertarian think tank
8. Canadian capital
9. Vital
10. Printed weather forecasters
11. Perjures oneself
12. Lightning unit
13. "Do go on . . ."
21. Expel
22. Toques and tams
25. Engulf
26. Ancient Aegean region
27. "Stones for Ibarra" author Harriet
28. Friend of Owl and Rabbit
29. Poem's final stanza
30. Nonfiction author Klein
31. Brave reply to "Any volunteers?"
32. Terrier type
37. Take on, like The Onion
39. Morn's antithesis
40. Have all one could ask for
43. ___-Japanese War
45. Italian lake
48. Cause to change
49. "Maybe later"
50. Reddish-brown
53. Pulitzer-winning Herman with "The Caine Mutiny"
54. ". . . baked in___"
55. Big name in espionage
56. List shortener
57. Target, for Target
58. Boxers and pugs, e.g.
59. Terrier type
60. Command ctrs.

Scare on the Air

70

JAMES SAJDAK

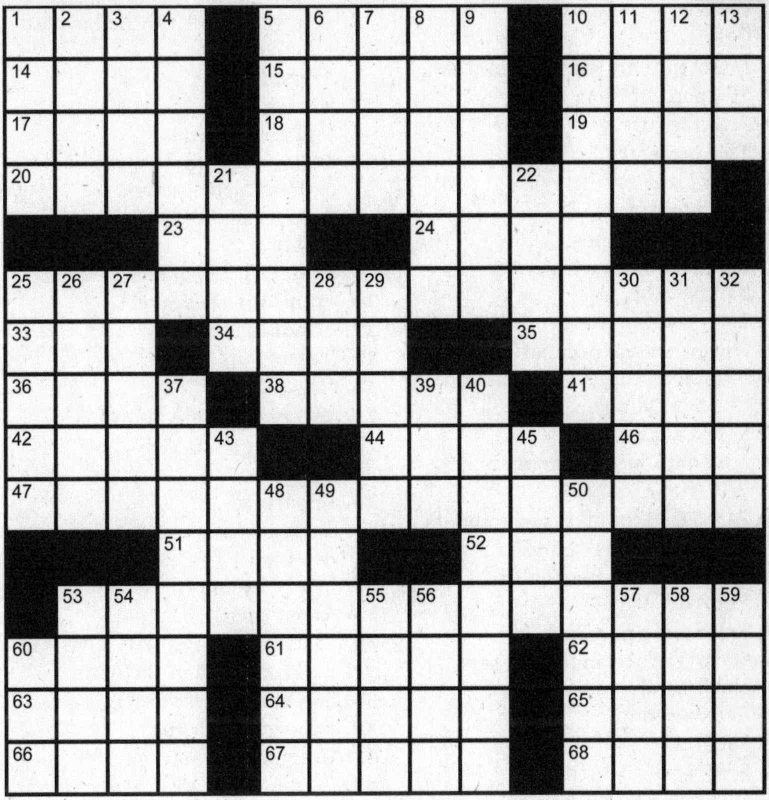

1 2 3 4 5 6 7 8 9 10 11 12 13
14 15 16
17 18 19
20 21 22
23 24
25 26 27 28 29 30 31 32
33 34 35
36 37 38 39 40 41
42 43 44 45 46
47 48 49 50
51 52
53 54 55 56 57 58 59
60 61 62
63 64 65
66 67 68

71

ACROSS

1. Important milieu for 67-Across
7. 100 percent
10. Enzyme suffixes
14. The Supremes' "___ Symphony"
15. BTW
16. Wind indicator
17. Causing weariness
18. Way of talking with one's hands?: Abbr.
19. Be ___ with (entertain)
20. One of several occupations for 67-Across
23. Chuckle syllable
25. Suffix with Caesar
26. Adequate, as an apartment
27. WWII side
29. Bad sound for bikers or campers
31. Maritime money handler
32. "I've Been Working on the Railroad" lady
34. Volunteer's phrase
36. 67-Across's term for the new black intellectual elite
40. Actors' group
41. Squalid
43. Forgoes one's turn
46. Dungeons & Dragons co.
48. Howard Hughes's old theaters
49. Northwestern potatoes
51. Bit of a draft
53. Class for some Mex.-Americans
54. Movement spearheaded by 67-Across
57. Flemish painter Jan van ___
58. Cold, like some receptions
59. Catches Z's
62. "Ain't ___ lucky one?"
63. Old 8-bit gaming console, for short
64. Like an environmentalist, slangily
65. Queen who wrote "Leap of Faith"
66. 0° long. hrs.
67. This puzzle's honoree

DOWN

1. String before K
2. Finger-snapper's shout
3. Cold War name for the People's Republic
4. Animal abode
5. Rubber duck–loving Muppet
6. Molten materials
7. "I'm not ___" (polite way of expressing distaste)
8. Brand that "disinfects to protect"
9. Swift's nation of small souls
10. Frank Sinatra's love
11. Gandhi's "sirs"
12. Isolate
13. "Irish" breed
21. Where originally found
22. Small eggs
23. Owned
24. Departure
28. Tableware item with holes in its head
30. Used a broom
33. About this
35. "Battleship Potemkin" city
37. Bull accessory in cartoons
38. Start of an instruction in a cab
39. Managed-care gps.
42. Designer monogram
43. Fill the room with, as recorded music
44. "What ___ be alive!"
45. Quixote's sidekick
47. Prepared to spit, say
50. Command to some attack dogs
52. Flavored rice dish
55. Sac
56. Balkan native
60. ___ Beta Kappa
61. Part of TBS: Abbr.

W.E.B. of Influence

T CAMPBELL

72

ACROSS

1. Flirt with
7. Highlander
11. Scheduling abbr.
14. Nancy in Washington, D.C.
15. Numbers subject
16. C++ or H+
17. Dr. Frankenstein's field of study?
19. "As if!"
20. "The Pied Piper of Hamelin" creature
21. Zone
22. Walrus weapons
24. Top-of-the-line
26. Get a laugh out of
28. Dr. Frankenstein's quick-turning hardware?
33. On the ___ (fleeing)
34. Spotted
35. Germanic tribesman
36. La Scala highlight
38. Regular: Abbr.
40. Prefix with "Cop," in a sci-fi film
41. "The 25th Annual ___ County Spelling Bee"
44. Back in the day
47. Fly trap
48. Dr. Frankenstein's treadmill class title?
51. Chaise cover, perhaps
52. Lincoln ___ (Lego alternative)
53. Kelly of "The West Wing"
55. Pitchers' figs.
57. "Scaaaaaary"
60. Frat facade letter
61. Dr. Frankenstein, e.g.?
65. German article
66. Like the White Rabbit in Wonderland
67. Like some saws and tires
68. Old PC platform
69. Greek matchmaker
70. Corrects, as text

DOWN

1. Radar's rank on "M*A*S*H": Abbr.
2. One with a fortune coming
3. It comes before "Bravo"
4. Morgue ID
5. ___ Enterprise ("Star Trek" vessel)
6. Spanish sauce whose name means "to prick"
7. Hook's right-hand man
8. Biblical promised land
9. Like some pharmaceuticals, for short
10. London metro
11. Hollywood, casually
12. It has a spine but no brain
13. Hill-building bugs
18. Dunne, Adler, and Rich
23. "Forgive ___ trespasses"
25. Quaker ___ (cereal)
27. Bus. drivers?
28. Lash who played the Cheyenne Kid
29. Cubic zirconia and margarine, e.g.
30. Being pulled behind
31. "Ain't Too Proud ___"
32. Pretentious person
33. Hollywood cops, for short
37. Choice words?
39. Site of some modern forensics work
42. Good-natured
43. Bad, in Barcelona
45. Finality
46. Cardiology readout: Abbr.
49. Must
50. Tristan's tryster
53. TV horse
54. Cincinnati's state
56. Breads with caraway seeds, often
58. Chief Viking god
59. Unit of cattle
62. Rowing tool
63. "___ Legend" (2007 Will Smith movie)
64. "Treasure Island" monogram

Just What the Doctor Ordered

PATRICK BLINDAUER AND REBECCA YOUNG

69. Scotch or masking material
70. Name of several Egyptian kings

ACROSS

1. TV show's most watched episode, often
7. Like some basements
11. Juan's "What?"
14. Like a sociopath
15. 1996 role for Gwyneth
16. Home of the Trojans
17. Heller novel about comparatively simple problems?
19. Words Romeo says to Juliet in front of Friar Lawrence
20. They've broken up
21. Quote, in a paper
22. Call to turn toward Mecca
23. Global: Abbr.
25. Nickname for a Houston Rockets superstar
28. Dumas novel about an early Musketeers reunion?
33. Walt Disney World city, briefly
34. High-___
35. "Let me give it a try"
37. Model Klum
39. ___City (computer game)
41. Personal boiling point
42. Digestion aid
44. Place where plastic surgery is done, often
46. Swan song
47. Dickens novel that doesn't cover much real estate, with "A"?
50. Drifting on a boat
51. Paul who wrote "She's a Lady"
52. Beatle Lennon
55. Diplomat's trait
57. Common video file format
61. "Simpsons" character who went to college in Calcutta
62. Event for bargain hunters, and this puzzle's theme
65. Henpeck
66. Tom Joad, e.g.
67. Delphic prophet
68. "Xanadu" band

DOWN

1. Deal with head-on
2. Science museum movie format
3. Musical unit
4. Inverse trig function
5. "Well, ___-di-dah!"
6. One who's been voted in
7. Chemical that bugs bugs
8. Soldier's org. founded in 1944
9. Married mlle.
10. Goat god
11. Class assessment
12. Fed. food inspectors
13. "Wealth of Nations" subj.
18. Flowers in a Whitman poem
22. When Rosencrantz and Guildenstern appear
24. "All the News That's Fit to Print" paper, for short
26. Avril follower
27. Ben of "Good Will Hunting"
28. Site of a 16th-century Catholic council
29. Fictional Doolittle
30. Horned African animal
31. M. ___ Walsh
32. Coming down outside
33. "___ sits high in all the people's hearts" (Shakespeare)
36. Abbr. on a pay stub
38. "Do not go gentle into that good night" poet Thomas
40. Monte Carlo's country
43. Classified letters
45. Requested via courier
48. Fight souvenir
49. 2001 film for which Sean Penn was nominated for a Best Actor Oscar
52. John Doe's partner
53. October birthstone
54. Boss on a designer label?
56. For ___ (if you pay)
58. D.C. lobbying grps.
59. Palindromic fashion magazine

Books on a Budget

JONATHAN PORAT

(crossword grid)

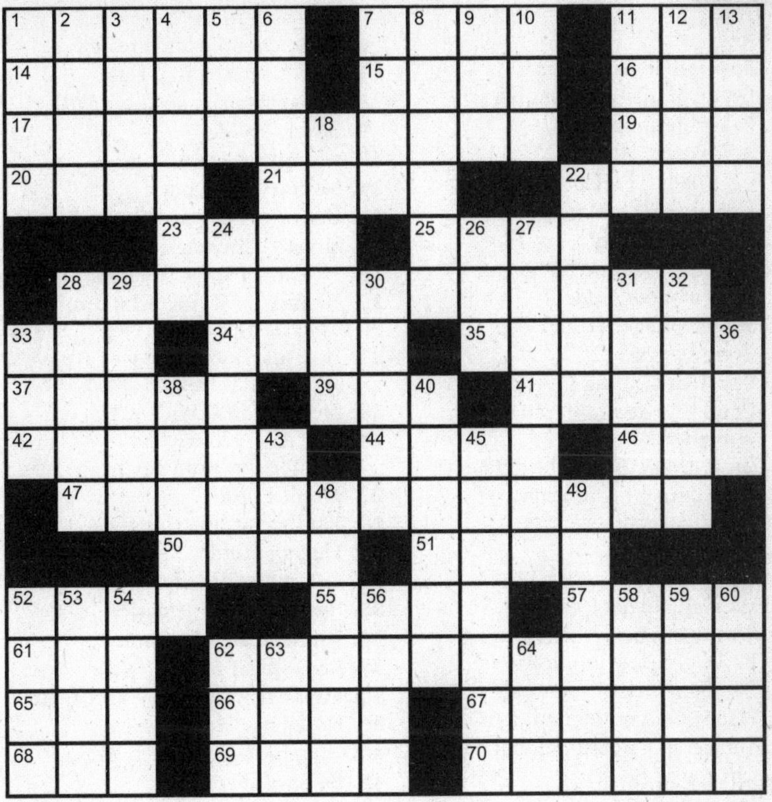

60. Thousands, in slang
62. Sizzling, say
63. Letters at the post office?
64. Monastic title

147

74

ACROSS

1. Position of leadership
5. Double-boiler heat source
10. Pale blue shade
14. AARP part: Abbr.
15. ___ Roadster (electric sports car)
16. Largest of the Mariana Islands
17. Dove's doctrine?
20. Widely used food plant
21. Type of med. student
22. Some nonagenarians
25. Good suffix?
26. Bay Area landing spot
29. Condition at a repressive university?
32. Govt. that created the Stasi
33. "Prospero ___ y felicidad" (seasonal lyric)
34. Smidgens
35. Army leaders
39. Windshield device
42. Test taken before submitting Ph.D. program applications
43. Big name in campgrounds
46. Happy bodybuilder's axiom?
51. Subject of a noted muscial ode
52. Clinton or Bush, e.g.
53. Prima ballerinas
54. Magazine publisher, e.g.
57. Jessica of "Sin City"
58. Source of information in Oceania, whose manipulations are this puzzle's theme
63. 1998 animated film
64. "The ___ Good Feelings" (Monroe's presidency)
65. Prefix with plane
66. Certain reed
67. Cheap Tata cars
68. States

DOWN

1. "The ___" (Leon Uris novel)
2. Ostrichlike bird
3. Cigarette ad claim
4. "The Wind in the Willows" character
5. Ralph who illustrated "Fear and Loathing in Las Vegas"
6. It's fermented and brewed
7. Suffix with opal or fluor
8. Social theorist de Tocqueville
9. Barbie builder
10. Antiquing agent
11. Military-style hut
12. Old Egypt-Syria alliance: Abbr.
13. Singer Winehouse
18. Feature of some funerals
19. "Drive, ___" (1971 film directed by Jack Nicholson)
22. Hammarskjöld who was Trygve's successor at the UN
23. Monk's condition, on TV
24. "Lift Every Voice and ___" (James Weldon Johnson poem)
27. Monk's title
28. Yiddish interjections
30. Flu symptom
31. Columnist Marilyn ___ Savant
35. Flying-south formation
36. "Gunsmoke" star James
37. R&B singer India ___
38. Fires everyone and starts again
39. Noted bus. daily
40. Olympic figure skater Midori
41. Be nosy about
43. Highly active Hawaiian volcano
44. Sugar suffix
45. Barnyard brayer
47. Source of some food allergies
48. Land, in South America
49. Run fast, so to speak
50. People born under the sign of the scales
55. You might get fitted to find yours
56. Hero Jack of Tom Clancy novels
58. Warhol subject
59. Dvořák's "Cello Concerto ___ Minor"
60. Game-winning tic-tac-toe line
61. Attempt
62. Seasonal laughs

Triumph of the Party

LEONARD WILLIAMS

75

ACROSS

1. Opens one's eyes
6. Welcome to the team
10. Choosy type
14. Exercise
15. "I smell ___!"
16. Actress Anderson
17. Tend
18. LeBlanc of "Friends"
19. Underling: Abbr.
20. Beginning of a quote by introverted author Logan Pearsall Smith
23. Franken and Gore
25. Be supine
26. Listening org.
27. Hooray for Jesus
28. Part 2 of the quote
31. More bassy
33. Hedge type
34. "The Fall of the House of ___"
36. Org. in search of aliens
37. Confess, archaically
39. Words to the captain
43. Whitman's dooryard bloomer
45. Secure again
47. Not as it should be
50. Part 3 of the quote
52. Hit with a dodgeball, say
53. Bigger than med.
55. Classicism or realism start
56. ___ de guerre
57. End of the quote
61. Commercial word to entice dieters
62. Key with 4 sharps
63. Loam and clay
66. "National Velvet" author Bagnold
67. Place with salas
68. One may be HD
69. Winos
70. Suffix meaning "name"
71. Region of the Sahara

DOWN

1. "Fantastic Mr. Fox" director Anderson
2. Lumberjack's tool
3. Stays in shape
4. Alias for the artist Romain de Tirtoff
5. Tattletale
6. Role for Kenneth Branagh
7. "Dies ___" (Latin hymn)
8. Teenager's room, often
9. Kett and James
10. Venetian blind piece
11. Missing person, of a sort
12. Discounted
13. Like coffee, often
21. Heat that's packed
22. Noah Webster's alma mater
23. European range
24. Former Milan money
29. Sins
30. Nagging feeling
32. Floss brand
35. Like unicorns
38. Big name in luxury pens
40. Not quite mature
41. Outer: Prefix
42. Milk option
44. Land in the ocean
46. Self-absorbed types
47. They can't be compared to oranges
48. Wool source
49. "No explanation needed"
51. Stuck
54. ___-Roman wrestling
58. Some government agents
59. A snap
60. PBS science series
64. Author Harper
65. Arch city: Abbr.

Just Give Me a Book

VERNA SUIT

SOLUTIONS

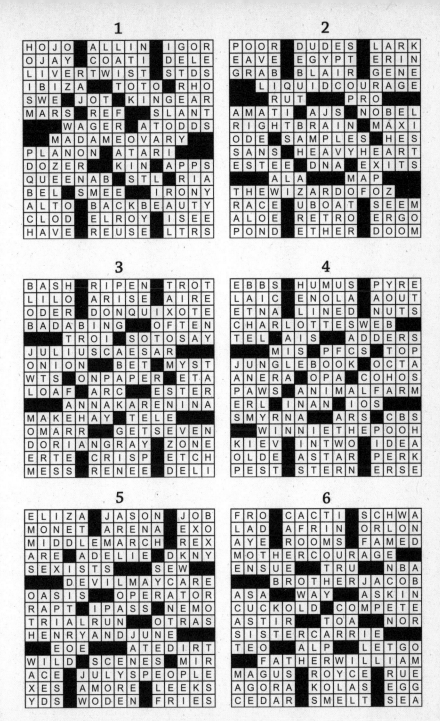

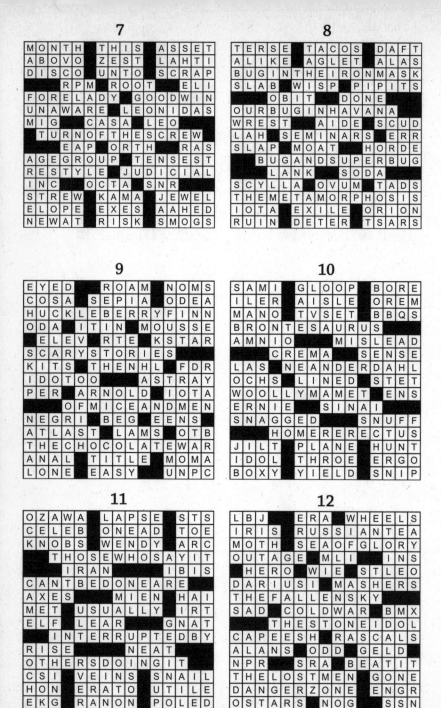

7

MONTH · THIS · ASSET
ABOVO · ZEST · LAHTI
DISCO · UNTO · SCRAP
· · RPM · ROOT · · ELI
FORELADY · GOODWIN
UNAWARE · LEONIDAS
MIG · CASA · LEO ·
· TURNOFTHESCREW
· EAP · ORTH · RAS
AGEGROUP · TENSEST
RESTYLE · JUDICIAL
INC · OCTA · SNR
STREW · KAMA · JEWEL
ELOPE · EXES · AAHED
NEWAT · RISK · SMOGS

8

TERSE · TACOS · DAFT
ALIKE · AGLET · ALAS
BUGINTHEIRONMASK
SLAB · WISP · PIPITS
· OBIT · DONE ·
OURBUGINHAVANA
WREST · AIDE · SCUD
LAH · SEMINARS · ERR
SLAP · MOAT · HORDE
· BUGANDSUPERBUG
· LANK · SODA ·
SCYLLA · OVUM · TADS
THEMETAMORPHOSIS
IOTA · EXILE · ORION
RUIN · DETER · TSARS

9

EYED · ROAM · NOMS
COSA · SEPIA · ODEA
HUCKLEBERRYFINN
ODA · ITIN · MOUSSE
· ELEV · RTE · KSTAR
SCARYSTORIES
KITS · THENHL · FDR
IDOTOO · ASTRAY
PER · ARNOLD · IOTA
· OFMICEANDMEN
NEGRI · BEG · EENS
ATLAST · LAMS · OTB
THECHOCOLATEWAR
ANAL · TITLE · MOMA
LONE · EASY · UNPC

10

SAMI · GLOOP · BORE
ILER · AISLE · OREM
MANO · TVSET · BBQS
BRONTESAURUS ·
AMNIO · · MISLEAD
· CREMA · SENSE
LAS · NEANDERDAHL
OCHS · LINED · STET
WOOLLYMAMET · ENS
ERNIE · SINAI ·
SNAGGED · SNUFF
· HOMERERECTUS
JILT · PLANE · HUNT
IDOL · THROE · ERGO
BOXY · YIELD · SNIP

11

OZAWA · LAPSE · STS
CELEB · ONEAD · TOE
KNOBS · WENDY · ARC
· THOSEWHOSAYIT
· IRAN · IBIS
CANTBEDONEARE ·
AXES · MIEN · HAI
MET · USUALLY · IRT
ELF · LEAR · GNAT
· INTERRUPTEDBY
RISE · NEAT ·
OTHERSDOINGIT
CSI · VEINS · SNAIL
HON · ERATO · UTILE
EKG · RANON · POLED

12

LBJ · ERA · WHEELS
IRIS · RUSSIANTEA
MOTH · SEAOFGLORY
OUTAGE · MLI · INS
· HERO · WIE · STLEO
DARIUSI · MASHERS
THEFALLENSKY ·
SAD · COLDWAR · BMX
· THESTONEIDOL
CAPEESH · RASCALS
ALANS · ODD · GELD
NPR · SRA · BEATIT
THELOSTMEN · GONE
DANGERZONE · ENGR
OSTARS · NOG · SSN

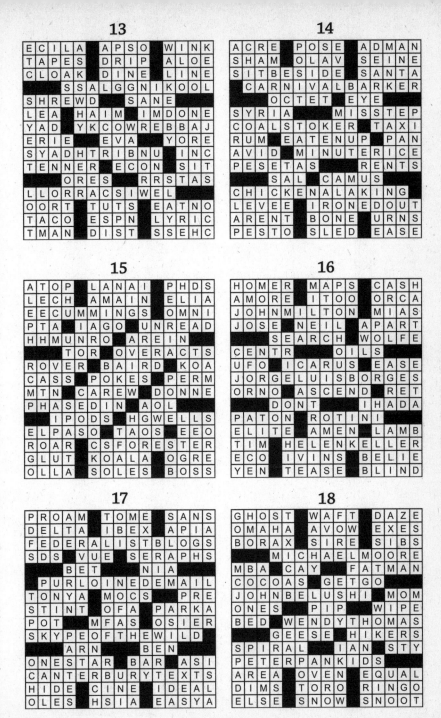

19

```
AMP  SWAP  AHS  JOLT
DIE  PICA  LOTHARIO
ENDZONES  CLEANSER
PORTNOYSCOMPLAINT
TROIS  GAT  NEE
   LORDOFTHEFLIES
COTERIE  OTOE
APU  OFMICEANDMEN
RANTS  ALI  ZAIRE
THEWASTELAND  NSW
   IDEE  APACHES
THEGREATGATSBY
YON  ODD  ONTAP
PRIDEANDPREJUDICE
INSOMNIA  OXONIANS
SELFTEST  IPOD  NET
TREF  WIE  TONS  TDS
```

20

```
CARS  MOJO  WRATH
TROT  ARES  HANOI
REBECCADEWINTER
LATERAL  ATTEST
   LAD  OGLES
LADYMACBETH  BOZ
ODED  MELS  ADELE
ADLAI  LIT  TEALS
FLINT  IGET  ALIT
SEA  ANNESHIRLEY
   GLUED  IDS
LCHAIM  UMLAUTS
ELIZABETHBENNET
AUDEN  VIOL  TINE
REEDS  ASHE  ATTN
```

21

```
GRASS  FLAG  TEAR
AORTA  RICO  ESPN
BONES  ENTO  LAPS
STEPHENDEDALUS
   MASC  BRA
KATO  THECYCLOPS
ADAM  ROE  LUAU
SAX  AMASS  INC
ENOS  MET  AJAR
MOLLYBLOOM  NAME
   OUR  BABY
THELOTUSEATERS
HAIG  SANE  SORBO
MXVI  IRIS  TWAIN
MIEN  APTS  ANTSY
```

22

```
BEGUN  SNEAD  BIB
ORONO  EAGLE  ADA
CRYINGWOOLF  COB
COAT  ISM  WEEKLY
ERSATZ  ICECAP
   SUMP  ATTRACT
BED  BORER  SLIMY
AROD  SILLS  SNIP
LINED  SLOTH  EXO
KENNELS  TABS
   ESSAYS  LOWFAT
MADEIT  AKA  ALEE
ONE  GETHIGHMARX
PTA  NSAID  OPCIT
EEL  STUBS  TYKES
```

23

```
STEP  BAA  SEALS
LAVA  TOSS  ORBIT
OXEN  ETHANFROME
TIRADE  POT  VOW
   MANET  RECESS
ANNAKARENINA
PEA  AGREE  SLAB
ERITREA  ARCHIVE
DOLE  TATER  REV
   MADAMEBOVARY
TRIPLE  PRONE
HEN  IAN  OYSTER
EFFI  BRIEST  SILO
FERMI  CPAS  EKED
TRAPS  EAT  LIME
```

24

```
BALLAD  MAAM  CAM
AGASSI  OSLO  OVO
LETUSGOTHEN  FAR
DDE  TETE  AFTA
   SILENTSEAS
RUSSETS  WARPERS
ASTOR  GENII
JALFREDPRUFROCK
   TOSCA  LILLI
MISTRAL  EMENDED
IMPOSSIBLE
APOP  OOLA  SMU
SAO  HUMANVOICES
MIN  EKES  INNATE
ARS  WENT  NECTAR
```

25

A	S	S	T		H	E	N	S			C	C	I	N	G
N	A	N	A		O	M	I	T			A	S	N	A	P
G	N	O	M	O	B	I	L	E			L	L	A	M	A
S	T	O	P	G	O			V	A	L	E				
T	A	T	E	R		T	H	E	R	E	W	I	L	L	
		R	E	T	R	O			T	R	I	V	I	A	
B	A	T	S		S	I	L	T			I	S	I	T	I
Y	M	A		B	E	B	L	O	O	D		E	R	R	
L	U	C	C	I		E	A	S	E		O	D	E	S	
A	S	I	A	G	O		N	E	R	T	S				
W	E	T	P	A	R	A	D	E		U	M	B	E	R	
			U	P	O	N			O	T	O	O	L	E	
S	C	A	L	P		T	H	E	J	U	N	G	L	E	
E	T	H	E	L		S	O	S	A		D	U	E	L	
C	R	A	T	E		Y	E	T	I		S	S	N	S	

26

W	H	E	N		O	R	E	S			P	S	H	A	W
H	E	R	O		R	A	V	E			I	C	O	M	E
A	R	I	D		S	T	A	N			C	A	N	I	D
M	A	N	S	F	I	E	L	D	B	A	R	K			
			A	N	D			A	S	A					
T	H	E	E	N	O	R	M	O	U	S	B	O	O	M	
R	U	L	E	S		A	L	D	O		S	P	A		
E	M	I	R		F	U	N	D	S		A	C	A	R	
A	P	T		P	A	S	S			O	F	A	R	C	
T	H	E	H	O	U	S	E	O	F	B	I	R	T	H	
			O	W	N			U	R	I					
	T	H	E	S	E	C	R	E	T	L	I	F	E		
A	P	O	O	R		D	O	M	E		E	N	O	L	
S	A	D	H	U		D	I	A	Z		O	F	B	S	
S	W	O	O	P		A	N	N	E		N	O	S	E	

27

G	M	C		C	A	S	B	A	H		T	A	D	A	
R	A	H		D	E	P	L	O	Y		I	R	O	N	
A	R	I		S	O	H	E	L	P	M	E	G	O	D	
S	Y	N	C		L	E	A		E	A	T	E	R	Y	
P	J	O	R	O	U	R	K	E		J	A	N			
		A	P	S	E		X	F	A	C	T	O	R		
H	O	W	I	E		V	I	E			I	K	E		
T	H	E	G	L	O	B	E	T	H	E	A	T	R	E	
T	I	N		H	E	X			B	R	E	A	K		
P	O	T	S	H	O	T		G	E	A	R				
		D	E	E		A	D	A	M	Y	A	U	C	H	
F	L	U	X	E	S		R	I	B		Y	M	H	A	
L	I	T	T	L	E	W	O	M	E	N		B	I	Z	
A	R	C	O		N	E	V	A	D	A		E	V	E	
K	A	H	N		T	E	E	N	S	Y		R	E	D	

28

S	V	E	N		E	A	S	E	D		S	W	A	P	
C	O	M	E		L	U	N	A	R		P	I	S	A	
A	T	E	E		P	T	E	R	O		I	N	K	Y	
L	E	N	D	S	A	H	E	L	P	I	N	G			
P	A	D		T	S	O			R	E	T	R	O		
E	Y	E	C	O	O	R	D	I	N	A	T	I	O	N	
L	E	D	T	O		I	S	O			P	O	E		
			A	D	A	M	S	M	I	T	H				
S	E	E		D	O	C			A	S	S	A	D		
S	E	C	O	N	D	B	O	O	K	S	T	O	R	E	
W	O	L	F	E			N	I	T		N	S	A		
	I	N	V	I	S	I	B	L	E	H	A	N	D		
T	Y	P	O		M	O	D	A	L		O	T	O	S	
O	U	S	T		P	U	L	S	E		W	A	V	E	
E	P	E	E		S	P	E	E	D		L	S	A	T	

29

R	A	S	H		Z	A	D	O	R	A		N	U	M	B	S
O	C	H	O		A	M	O	R	E	S		A	T	I	L	T
T	H	E	B	I	G	P	E	E	L	S		V	A	L	O	R
C	Y	B	O	R	G			I	C	Y		A	T	E		
			K	E	T	T		I	S	O		A	N	T	E	
	T	H	E	D	R	O	W	N	I	N	G	L	O	O	P	
C	L	O	U	D		I	R	A	N		F	O	P			
Y	A	K	S		F	A	R	R		K	E	B		B	M	X
T	H	E	K	I	L	L	E	R	I	N	S	I	D	E	E	M
E	R	N		N	A	S		I	R	I	S		I	N	G	E
		E	D	U		H	O	A	G		S	E	D	A	N	
E	V	I	L	U	N	D	E	R	T	H	E	N	U	S		
R	O	X	Y		T	E	X		E	T	R	E				
M	R	T		C	S	A			V	E	R	I	T	E		
I	T	A	L	O		T	H	E	T	H	I	R	D	N	A	M
N	E	P	A	L		H	A	R	K	E	N		A	T	O	M
E	X	A	C	T		S	T	R	O	N	G		S	O	S	A

30

H	I	D		J	A	B	S		Q	B	S		T	R	I
I	D	A	R	E	Y	O	U		U	R	I		A	I	T
S	A	M	E	N	E	S	S		A	I	M		R	G	S
	A	N	A	R	C	H	I	S	M	I	S	T	H	E	
F	O	G	G			I	R	A		N	A	T	L		
G	R	E	A	T	L	I	B	E	R	A	T	O	R	O	F
S	O	S		I	A	M	A			S	O	R	E	N	
		M	A	N	F	R	O	M	T	H	E				
	T	B	O	N	D		A	E	R	I		V	I	P	
P	H	A	N	T	O	M	S	T	H	A	T	H	A	V	E
S	E	L	A		A	E	C			A	N	E	W		
H	E	L	D	H	I	M	C	A	P	T	I	V	E		
A	D	O		A	B	M		K	E	E	N	E	Y	E	D
W	G	N		R	E	A		E	N	C	I	R	C	L	E
S	E	E		M	X	L		S	A	S	S		K	I	N

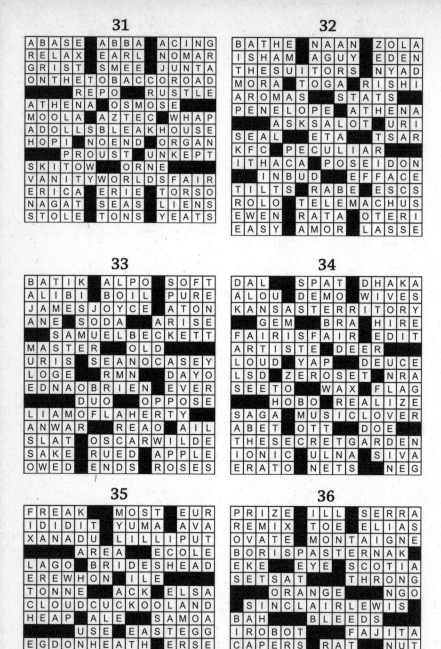

31

```
ABASE ABBA  ACING
RELAX EARL  NOMAR
GRIST SMEE  JUNTA
ONTHETOBACCOROAD
      REPO  RUSTLE
ATHENA OSMOSE
MOOLA AZTEC WHAP
ADOLLSBLEAKHOUSE
HOPI NOEND ORGAN
    PROUST UNKEPT
SKITOW ORNE
VANITYWORLDSFAIR
ERICA ERIE TORSO
NAGAT SEAS LIENS
STOLE TONS YEATS
```

32

```
BATHE NAAN  ZOLA
ISHAM AGUY  EDEN
THESUITORS  NYAD
MORA TOGA  RISHI
AROMAS  STATS
PENELOPE ATHENA
  ASKSALOT  URI
SEAL  ETA  TSAR
KFC  PECULIAR
ITHACA POSEIDON
  INBUD  EFFACE
TILTS RABE  ESCS
ROLO TELEMACHUS
EWEN RATA  OTERI
EASY AMOR  LASSE
```

33

```
BATIK ALPO  SOFT
ALIBI BOIL  PURE
JAMESJOYCE  ATON
ANE SODA  ARISE
  SAMUELBECKETT
MASTER  OLD
URIS SEANOCASEY
LOGE RMN  DAYO
EDNAOBRIEN EVER
   DUO  OPPOSE
LIAMOFLAHERTY
ANWAR REAO  AIL
SLAT OSCARWILDE
SAKE RUED APPLE
OWED ENDS ROSES
```

34

```
DAL  SPAT  DHAKA
ALOU DEMO  WIVES
KANSASTERRITORY
  GEM  BRA HIRE
FAIRISFAIR EDIT
ARTISTE DEER
LOUD YAP  DEUCE
LSD ZEROSET NRA
SEETO WAX  FLAG
  HOBO REALIZE
SAGA MUSICLOVER
ABET OTT  DOE
THESECRETGARDEN
IONIC ULNA  SIVA
ERATO NETS  NEG
```

35

```
FREAK MOST  EUR
IDIDIT YUMA AVA
XANADU LILLIPUT
  AREA  ECOLE
LAGO BRIDESHEAD
EREWHON ILE
TONNE ACK  ELSA
CLOUDCUCKOOLAND
HEAP ALE  SAMOA
   USE EASTEGG
EGDONHEATH ERSE
ARIES  LAID
TOADHALL GILEAD
MAN OJAI HAIRDO
ENE DAWN LEASE
```

36

```
PRIZE ILL  SERRA
REMIX TOE  ELIAS
OVATE MONTAIGNE
BORISPASTERNAK
EKE  EYE SCOTIA
SETSAT THRONG
  ORANGE  NGO
SINCLAIRLEWIS
BAH  BLEEDS
IROBOT FAJITA
CAPERS RAT NUT
JEANPAULSARTRE
CENTESIMO LEONA
AVOIR DOH ANTIS
DOTTY ERA NOONE
```

37

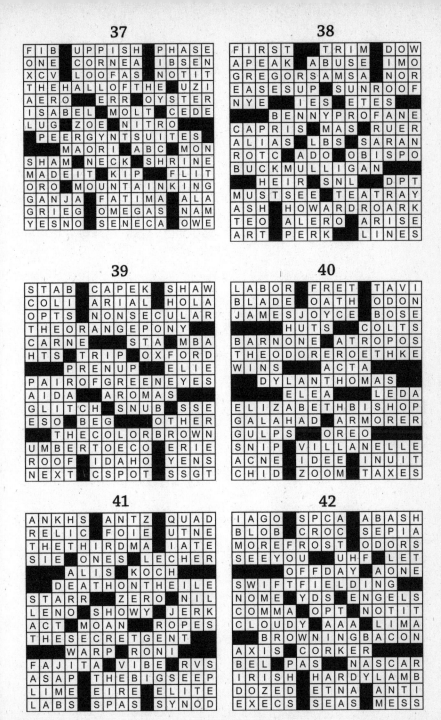

F	I	B		U	P	P	I	S	H		P	H	A	S	E
O	N	E		C	O	R	N	E	A		I	B	S	E	N
X	C	V		L	O	O	F	A	S		N	O	T	I	T
T	H	E	H	A	L	L	O	F	T	H	E		U	Z	I
A	E	R	O		E	R	R		O	Y	S	T	E	R	
I	S	A	B	E	L		M	O	L	T		C	E	D	E
L	U	G		Z	O	E		N	I	T	R	O			
	P	E	E	R	G	Y	N	T	S	U	I	T	E	S	
		M	A	O	R	I		A	B	C		M	O	N	
S	H	A	M		N	E	C	K		S	H	R	I	N	E
M	A	D	E	I	T		K	I	P		F	L	I	T	
O	R	O		M	O	U	N	T	A	I	N	K	I	N	G
G	A	N	J	A		F	A	T	I	M	A		A	L	A
G	R	I	E	G		O	M	E	G	A	S		N	A	M
Y	E	S	N	O		S	E	N	E	C	A		O	W	E

38

F	I	R	S	T		T	R	I	M		D	O	W
A	P	E	A	K		A	B	U	S	E		I	M	O
G	R	E	G	O	R	S	A	M	S	A		N	O	R
E	A	S	E	S	U	P		S	U	N	R	O	O	F
N	Y	E			I	E	S		E	T	E	S		
			B	E	N	N	Y	P	R	O	F	A	N	E
C	A	P	R	I	S		M	A	S		R	U	E	R
A	L	I	A	S		L	B	S		S	A	R	A	N
R	O	T	C		A	D	O		O	B	I	S	P	O
B	U	C	K	M	U	L	L	I	G	A	N			
	H	E	I	R		S	N	L		D	P	T		
M	U	S	T	S	E	E		T	E	A	T	R	A	Y
A	S	H		H	O	W	A	R	D	R	O	A	R	K
T	E	O		A	L	E	R	O		A	R	I	S	E
A	R	T		P	E	R	K		L	I	N	E	S	

39

S	T	A	B		C	A	P	E	K		S	H	A	W
C	O	L	I		A	R	I	A	L		H	O	L	A
O	P	T	S		N	O	N	S	E	C	U	L	A	R
T	H	E	O	R	A	N	G	E	P	O	N	Y		
C	A	R	N	E			S	T	A		M	B	A	
H	T	S		T	R	I	P		O	X	F	O	R	D
		P	R	E	N	U	P			E	L	I	E	
P	A	I	R	O	F	G	R	E	E	N	E	Y	E	S
A	I	D	A		A	R	O	M	A	S				
G	L	I	T	C	H		S	N	U	B		S	S	E
E	S	O		B	E	G			O	T	H	E	R	
	T	H	E	C	O	L	O	R	B	R	O	W	N	
U	M	B	E	R	T	O	E	C	O		E	R	I	E
R	O	O	F		I	D	A	H	O		Y	E	N	S
N	E	X	T		C	S	P	O	T		S	S	G	T

40

L	A	B	O	R		F	R	E	T		T	A	V	I
B	L	A	D	E		O	A	T	H		O	D	O	N
J	A	M	E	S	J	O	Y	C	E		B	O	S	E
		H	U	T	S			C	O	L	T	S		
B	A	R	N	O	N	E		A	T	R	O	P	O	S
T	H	E	O	D	O	R	E	R	O	E	T	H	K	E
W	I	N	S			A	C	T	A					
	D	Y	L	A	N	T	H	O	M	A	S			
		E	L	E	A					L	E	D	A	
E	L	I	Z	A	B	E	T	H	B	I	S	H	O	P
G	A	L	A	H	A	D		A	R	M	O	R	E	R
G	U	L	P	S		O	R	E	O					
S	N	I	P		V	I	L	L	A	N	E	L	L	E
A	C	N	E		I	D	E	E		I	N	U	I	T
C	H	I	D		Z	O	O	M		T	A	X	E	S

41

A	N	K	H	S		A	N	T	Z		Q	U	A	D
R	E	L	I	C		F	O	I	E		U	T	N	E
T	H	E	T	H	I	R	D	M	A		I	A	T	E
S	I	E		O	N	E	S		L	E	C	H	E	R
		A	L	I	S			K	O	C	H			
	D	E	A	T	H	O	N	T	H	E	I	L	E	
S	T	A	R	R		Z	E	R	O		N	I	L	
L	E	N	O		S	H	O	W	Y		J	E	R	K
A	C	T		M	O	A	N			R	O	P	E	S
T	H	E	S	E	C	R	E	T	G	E	N	T		
		W	A	R	P		R	O	N	I				
F	A	J	I	T	A		V	I	B	E		R	V	S
A	S	A	P		T	H	E	B	I	G	S	E	E	P
L	I	M	E		E	I	R	E		E	L	I	T	E
L	A	B	S		S	P	A	S		S	Y	N	O	D

42

I	A	G	O		S	P	C	A		A	B	A	S	H
B	L	O	B		C	R	O	C		S	E	P	I	A
M	O	R	E	F	R	O	S	T		O	D	O	R	S
S	E	E	Y	O	U			U	H	F		L	E	T
			O	F	F	D	A	Y		A	O	N	E	
S	W	I	F	T	F	I	E	L	D	I	N	G		
N	O	M	E		Y	D	S		E	N	G	E	L	S
C	O	M	M	A		O	P	T		N	O	T	I	T
C	L	O	U	D	Y		A	A	A		L	I	M	A
	B	R	O	W	N	I	N	G	B	A	C	O	N	
A	X	I	S		C	O	R	K	E	R				
B	E	L		P	A	S			N	A	S	C	A	R
I	R	I	S	H		H	A	R	D	Y	L	A	M	B
D	O	Z	E	D		E	T	N	A		A	N	T	I
E	X	E	C	S		S	E	A	S		M	E	S	S

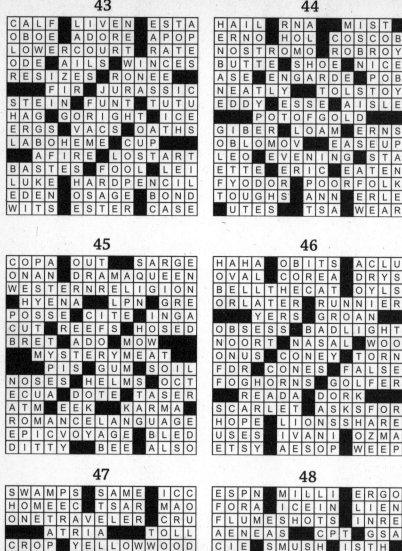

43

C	A	L	F	■	L	I	V	E	N	■	E	S	T	A
O	B	O	E	■	A	D	O	R	E	■	A	P	O	P
L	O	W	E	R	C	O	U	R	T	■	R	A	T	E
O	D	E	■	A	I	L	S	■	W	I	N	C	E	S
R	E	S	I	Z	E	S	■	R	O	N	E	E	■	■
■	■	F	I	R	■	J	U	R	A	S	S	I	C	■
S	T	E	I	N	■	F	U	N	T	■	T	U	T	U
H	A	G	■	G	O	R	I	G	H	T	■	I	C	E
E	R	G	S	■	V	A	C	S	■	O	A	T	H	S
L	A	B	O	H	E	M	E	■	C	U	P	■	■	■
■	A	F	I	R	E	■	L	O	S	T	A	R	T	■
B	A	S	T	E	S	■	F	O	O	L	■	L	E	I
L	U	K	E	■	H	A	R	D	P	E	N	C	I	L
E	D	E	N	■	O	S	A	G	E	■	B	O	N	D
W	I	T	S	■	E	S	T	E	R	■	C	A	S	E

44

H	A	I	L	■	R	N	A	■	M	I	S	T	■	■
E	R	N	O	■	H	O	L	■	C	O	S	C	O	B
N	O	S	T	R	O	M	O	■	R	O	B	R	O	Y
B	U	T	T	E	■	S	H	O	E	■	N	I	C	E
A	S	E	■	E	N	G	A	R	D	E	■	P	O	B
N	E	A	T	L	Y	■	T	O	L	S	T	O	Y	■
E	D	D	Y	■	E	S	S	E	■	A	I	S	L	E
■	■	P	O	T	O	F	G	O	L	D	■	■	■	■
G	I	B	E	R	■	L	O	A	M	■	E	R	N	S
O	B	L	O	M	O	V	■	E	A	S	E	U	P	■
L	E	O	■	E	V	E	N	I	N	G	■	S	T	A
E	T	T	E	■	E	R	I	C	■	E	A	T	E	N
F	Y	O	D	O	R	■	P	O	O	R	F	O	L	K
T	O	U	G	H	S	■	A	N	N	■	E	R	L	E
■	U	T	E	S	■	T	S	A	■	W	E	A	R	■

45

C	O	P	A	■	O	U	T	■	S	A	R	G	E	■
O	N	A	N	■	D	R	A	M	A	Q	U	E	E	N
W	E	S	T	E	R	N	R	E	L	I	G	I	O	N
■	H	Y	E	N	A	■	L	P	N	■	G	R	E	■
P	O	S	S	E	■	C	I	T	E	■	I	N	G	A
C	U	T	■	R	E	E	F	S	■	H	O	S	E	D
B	R	E	T	■	A	D	O	■	M	O	W	■	■	■
■	■	M	Y	S	T	E	R	Y	M	E	A	T	■	■
■	■	■	P	I	S	■	G	U	M	■	S	O	I	L
N	O	S	E	S	■	H	E	L	M	S	■	O	C	T
E	C	U	A	■	D	O	T	E	■	T	A	S	E	R
A	T	M	■	E	E	K	■	K	A	R	M	A	■	■
R	O	M	A	N	C	E	L	A	N	G	U	A	G	E
E	P	I	C	V	O	Y	A	G	E	■	B	L	E	D
D	I	T	T	Y	■	B	E	E	■	A	L	S	O	■

46

H	A	H	A	■	O	B	I	T	S	■	A	C	L	U
O	V	A	L	■	C	O	R	E	A	■	D	R	Y	S
B	E	L	L	T	H	E	C	A	T	■	O	Y	L	S
O	R	L	A	T	E	R	■	R	U	N	N	I	E	R
■	■	Y	E	R	S	■	G	R	O	A	N	■	■	■
O	B	S	E	S	S	■	B	A	D	L	I	G	H	T
N	O	O	R	T	■	N	A	S	A	L	■	W	O	O
O	N	U	S	■	C	O	N	E	Y	■	T	O	R	N
F	D	R	■	C	O	N	E	S	■	F	A	L	S	E
F	O	G	H	O	R	N	S	■	G	O	L	F	E	R
■	■	R	E	A	D	A	■	D	O	R	K	■	■	■
S	C	A	R	L	E	T	■	A	S	K	S	F	O	R
H	O	P	E	■	L	I	O	N	S	S	H	A	R	E
U	S	E	S	■	I	V	A	N	I	■	O	Z	M	A
E	T	S	Y	■	A	E	S	O	P	■	W	E	E	P

47

S	W	A	M	P	S	■	S	A	M	E	■	I	C	C
H	O	M	E	E	C	■	T	S	A	R	■	M	A	O
O	N	E	T	R	A	V	E	L	E	R	■	C	R	U
■	■	■	A	T	R	I	A	■	■	T	O	L	L	■
C	R	O	P	■	Y	E	L	L	O	W	W	O	O	D
O	U	G	H	T	■	■	I	R	A	I	L	S	■	■
S	T	R	O	H	S	■	A	L	A	I	■	■	■	■
T	H	E	R	O	A	D	N	O	T	T	A	K	E	N
■	■	■	U	R	I	S	■	E	U	D	O	R	A	■
■	S	L	U	G	G	O	■	■	P	A	B	S	T	■
A	N	O	T	H	E	R	D	A	Y	■	M	E	T	E
N	A	V	E	■	O	R	E	O	S	■	■	■	■	■
D	I	E	■	R	O	B	E	R	T	F	R	O	S	T
B	L	Y	■	E	A	R	S	■	I	S	I	D	O	R
E	S	A	■	A	T	R	A	■	S	T	B	E	D	E

48

E	S	P	N	■	M	I	L	L	I	■	E	R	G	O
F	O	R	A	■	I	C	E	I	N	■	L	I	E	N
F	L	U	M	E	S	H	O	T	S	■	I	N	R	E
A	E	N	E	A	S	■	C	P	T	■	G	S	A	■
C	I	E	■	S	M	U	S	H	■	I	S	T	H	■
E	L	R	O	Y	■	C	H	I	M	E	T	O	W	N
■	■	D	A	R	L	A	■	I	R	O	N	I	C	■
P	R	E	D	■	E	A	T	M	E	■	K	E	N	O
D	O	R	I	A	N	■	T	E	N	S	E	■	■	■
F	O	R	T	M	E	L	E	E	■	E	R	A	T	O
■	M	A	Y	I	■	A	R	K	I	N	■	S	E	X
L	M	N	■	D	O	Z	■	■	A	S	T	L	E	Y
O	A	T	H	■	K	I	N	G	M	E	K	O	N	G
O	T	R	A	■	R	E	A	R	S	■	O	P	I	E
K	E	Y	S	■	A	R	T	O	O	■	S	E	E	N

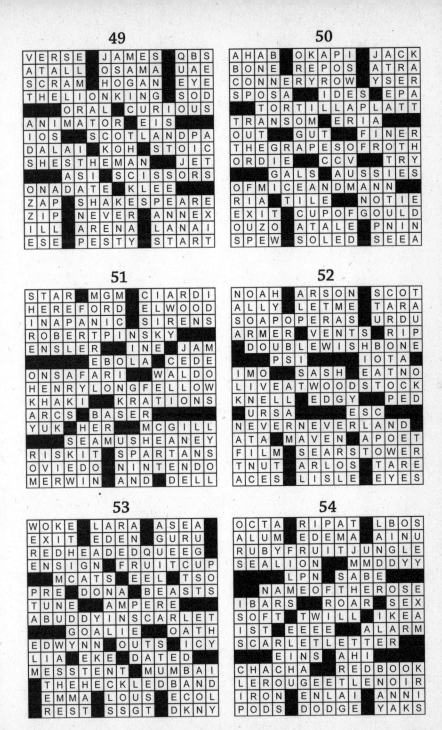

55

```
E D G E D . P A S D E . C O W
W E A V E . D I K E S . H U H
O U T O F A F R I C A . E R A
K T E L . U S E T O . I E S T
. . V A T . O D O R S . . .
. T H E L O S T W E E K E N D
A R A . E E R O . D E C O R
B A N A . D A R Y L . D A T E
B I D E T . S O U S . K I D
A L L T H E K I N G S M E N .
. E N D U E . O N A .
T U B A . G L U E S . N A I F
E V A . B E S T P I C T U R E
E E R . O N E N O . A E R I E
M A S . K E Y E S . B L A S T
```

56

```
P E N D . S A N E R . L B A R
O W I E . K N I F E . O R W E
G O N E W I T H T H E W A N D
O K A P I . . S A U C I E R
. . E L I Z A . B R A N D Y
F A N N Y H E L L . E L S
A X E D . O N D E C K . T A J
M E W . A P I . V I A . O L A
E L F . N E T M E N . P R O M
. A F T . H A R D T O M E S
D I N A H S . A S Y O U
E G G D R O P . . F L A M E
T A L E O F T W O C U T I E S
E V E R . A U D R A . R D A S
R E D S . R I S K Y . Y A L E
```

57

```
M E E T . O H S . P E R U
A T L A S . L E E S . O D O R
C A S S A N D R A W I L S O N
S L E E V E . O L I V E .
. R O P E . U N O . I R A
C C C . R H E A P E R L M A N
H A R D S E L L . Y U P I K
A R E A . W Y A T T . L E D A
C R O N E . M A R A U D E R
H E L E N T H O M A S . E R A
A Y E . R H O . P U T T .
. T O R T E . M R H Y D E
D A P H N E D U M A U R I E R
A I D A . W O R T . D O P E S
B R A N . G O V . B E D E
```

58

```
A L A R M . B L A B . S I R S
D A R E I . R I S E . A N E W
O P E N S . A R K S . I L I E
. T H E W A S T E L A N D
L S T . M A N . B R O W S E
A O R T A S . B Y E A R .
M A I N S T R E E T . D A R
B R O T H . A R G . F I E R O
S S S . T H E G O L D B U G
. W R E S T . R U S T L E
E S P I E S . H I S . S E T
T W E L F T H N I G H T
H I L L . L O O T . O H G E E
O R E O . A L U M . T E R R Y
S L E W . B A N E . S E R G E
```

59

```
J O A D . Z I N E . S H A R D
A U R A . E T O N . W A G E R
M R C Y P R E S S . E R A S E
A S H . R O M E . B E V I E S
. E P E E S . P A T E N T S
H O N E Y S . G I R L Y .
O D E T S . C A N D Y B A R
T O M E . K O T O S . I T I S
. M Y R M I D O N . T R A C E
. Q A T A R . T U C S O N
R E S U L T S . N I G H T .
E N T I T Y . P I C A . R I O
A T O N E . B U C K T H O R N
C R O C S . A C H E . O K A Y
T E P E E . D E E R . G E N X
```

60

```
A F E W . J F K . H O T T U B
M A K E . E E E . E R R A T A
P R E A C H E R . S E A M A N
. L O U T I S H . A H A
F O N T S . . G E N E R A L
A R C H I T E C T . A L A N
D E A . I L L . F R O
. M A T H E M A T I C I A N
. O A R . I A N . L O P
. T I N T . E M B E Z Z L E R
S U R G E O N . . I T A L Y
A V A . R O S S I N I
W A I T E R . L A W C L E R K
I L L I N I . A M I . E L H I
T U S C A N . B E N . S K E D
```

61

D	E	B	T	■	S	C	O	F	F	■	S	T	E	W
C	L	E	O	■	E	R	R	O	R	■	T	H	A	I
C	L	A	Y	■	R	A	B	B	I	T	E	A	R	S
A	I	R	■	W	E	B	S	■	J	O	A	N	N	E
B	E	M	O	A	N	S	■	Z	O	O	M	■	■	■
■	■	A	P	S	E	■	B	E	L	L	Y	F	U	L
S	T	R	I	P	■	P	A	L	E	S	■	O	N	O
H	I	K	E	■	W	O	R	D	S	■	A	X	I	S
I	V	E	■	S	H	E	B	A	■	B	U	T	T	E
P	O	T	S	H	O	T	S	■	R	U	D	E	■	■
■	■	■	T	I	C	S	■	N	O	G	I	R	L	S
O	K	S	A	N	A	■	I	O	U	S	■	R	A	T
U	N	C	L	E	R	E	M	U	S	■	A	I	D	E
T	E	A	K	■	E	R	A	S	E	■	P	E	L	E
S	E	T	S	■	S	A	X	E	S	■	B	R	E	R

62

G	A	P	S	■	K	A	N	G	A	■	C	L	A	Y
A	M	A	H	■	I	N	T	E	L	■	H	O	S	E
R	O	S	Y	■	D	O	S	E	S	■	O	O	P	S
B	U	D	D	A	N	D	B	R	O	O	K	S	■	■
O	R	E	I	D	A	■	■	■	B	E	E	T	S	■
■	■	■	E	P	I	T	O	M	E	■	L	A	I	■
P	E	S	O	S	■	M	O	P	E	Y	T	I	C	K
E	T	T	U	■	A	P	N	E	A	■	O	P	I	E
C	H	A	I	N	H	E	I	R	■	I	N	S	T	S
O	A	T	■	O	I	L	C	A	N	S	■	■	■	■
S	N	E	E	R	■	■	■	O	M	E	R	T	A	■
■	F	R	A	N	K	A	N	D	S	T	E	I	N	■
S	C	A	N	■	C	E	L	I	E	■	H	E	R	D
Q	E	I	I	I	■	A	R	E	N	A	■	E	V	E	R
S	O	R	E	■	A	R	E	A	L	■	L	E	S	E

63

I	Q	S	■	P	A	R	T	V	I	■	K	A	R	L
S	U	I	■	A	R	C	H	O	N	■	I	L	I	A
L	I	D	■	P	E	A	R	L	H	A	R	B	O	R
I	L	E	T	■	O	V	E	R	■	S	T	D	■	■
P	L	A	S	T	E	R	B	O	A	R	D	■	■	■
■	■	A	E	R	O	■	S	T	A	R	T	O	F	■
A	V	E	R	S	E	T	O	■	■	E	U	R	O	■
D	I	V	I	S	I	O	N	O	F	L	A	B	O	R
I	C	A	N	■	O	N	R	E	M	A	N	D	■	■
P	I	C	A	S	S	O	■	E	I	N	E	■	■	■
■	■	S	E	L	F	A	B	S	O	R	B	E	D	■
G	P	S	■	R	A	Y	S	■	■	S	O	L	O	■
L	A	T	E	B	L	O	O	M	E	R	■	W	I	Z
U	S	A	F	■	O	R	D	A	I	N	■	T	H	E
M	A	R	X	■	M	E	D	U	S	A	■	O	U	R

64

N	O	M	D	E	■	L	O	G	O	N	■	S	O	S
C	H	O	R	E	■	A	L	E	R	O	■	A	T	T
I	S	A	A	C	A	S	I	M	O	V	■	U	T	A
S	O	N	G	■	G	E	O	■	M	A	S	T	E	R
■	O	V	E	R	S	E	E	■	P	E	R	K	■	■
B	O	R	N	E	O	■	■	D	O	T	E	■	■	■
A	B	E	■	E	U	R	O	S	■	I	L	L	B	E
R	O	B	E	R	T	A	H	E	I	N	L	E	I	N
B	E	A	L	E	■	N	O	L	T	E	■	G	O	D
■	■	I	D	D	O	■	■	H	A	G	G	L	E	■
A	R	E	S	■	E	N	S	N	A	R	L	■	■	■
B	E	R	E	F	T	■	A	E	C	■	O	T	O	S
A	L	A	■	R	A	Y	B	R	A	D	B	U	R	Y
T	A	S	■	Y	I	E	L	D	■	E	A	T	E	N
E	Y	E	■	E	L	W	E	S	■	P	L	U	M	E

65

A	D	D	■	U	M	A	■	I	S	M	■	P	M	S
T	A	R	■	C	A	N	■	R	C	A	■	R	A	U
T	H	E	R	O	A	D	■	A	R	D	U	O	U	S
A	L	I	E	N	■	Q	U	E	S	E	R	A	■	■
■	■	I	N	V	I	S	I	B	L	E	M	A	N	■
S	C	A	N	■	A	M	I	■	S	E	D	■	■	■
I	O	S	■	A	L	A	N	A	■	I	C	O	N	S
G	R	E	E	N	E	G	G	S	A	N	D	H	A	M
H	Y	A	T	T	■	E	L	O	P	E	■	S	T	U
■	■	O	I	L	■	E	R	S	■	W	O	O	T	■
F	R	A	N	K	E	N	S	T	E	I	N	■	■	■
R	E	R	I	N	S	E	■	■	O	B	A	M	A	■
I	C	E	C	O	L	D	■	U	N	N	A	M	E	D
E	T	A	■	C	I	D	■	M	R	I	■	P	E	Z
D	O	S	■	K	E	A	■	P	A	C	■	S	T	E

66

C	E	L	■	T	R	A	M	P	■	M	I	S	S	M
O	V	I	■	H	E	L	I	O	■	A	N	T	I	C
G	E	O	■	I	N	O	N	U	■	I	R	A	N	I
I	N	T	H	E	T	W	I	N	K	L	I	N	G	■
T	I	T	O	V	■	S	D	I	■	■	D	S	L	■
O	F	A	N	E	Y	E	■	T	O	M	A	T	O	■
■	■	■	E	L	S	E	■	B	A	R	O	N	■	■
■	L	O	V	E	I	S	B	L	I	N	D	■	■	■
O	P	E	R	A	■	S	A	R	I	■	■	■	■	■
L	A	M	E	N	T	■	■	O	F	F	L	E	S	H
E	N	O	■	O	I	L	■	E	A	R	T	O	■	■
■	A	N	O	A	T	H	I	N	H	E	A	V	E	N
I	C	A	L	L	■	A	B	O	I	L	■	I	R	K
M	E	D	A	L	■	V	E	R	V	E	■	N	E	E
S	A	E	N	S	■	E	L	M	E	R	■	G	O	D

67

```
C H E Z   S L A P   U D O N
A G R A   H E R A   N I T A
T H E G R E A T J O W E T T
    A Y E   A R A M A I C
T H E T E N T H M A N   W O E
W A S       A A A   T H A N E
A L P S   U R N   F E E
  E N G L A N D M A D E M E
    T E E   S I N   L E V I
T O A S T   J I F   S E C
S I S   A G U N F O R S A L E
A L K A L I S     S E A
  E N D O F T H E A F F A I R
  R O A N   I M O K   E C R U
  S T Y E   N O N A   R E S T
```

68

```
E T A S   N A S A L   O H M S
R U N T   O N I C E   R O M A
E X T E N U A T E D   A M I D
  I V A N T U R G E N E V
R A S E D       B E R G
A Z O   A P I E     Y E O H
J A C K L O N D O N   T Z A R
A L I I   O M E G A   E Y R E
H E A D   H E N R Y J A M E S
  A L S O   S E S E   A M E
    I N S P     E R N S T
  J O S E P H C O N R A D
W A L T   A I R C U S H I O N
I N G E   S L A T Y   A A R E
G E A R   M E M O S   L S A T
```

69

```
J A P A N   A S S E T   P A P A
A M I T A   R E H O E   A L E C
D O N H O   E L I S A   N A S H
A R T E M I S A P H R O D I T E
    N I N A     E S A I
C H I A   E T H I C   H O N O R
L U T Z   P L A N A   U N A M I
A M I E   T A I N T S   Y V E S
N O N U S   S T E E L   S A G E
G R A S P   A I S H A   U L A N
    H E A P     E S T S
H E R A C R O N U S H E R M E S
G L A D   A L E R T   R H O D Y
T I G E   B L I N I   R E S I N
V E E S   S O L E A   Y A T E S
```

70

```
C D L I   B A C O N   A L B A
Z O O M   O V A T E   L I O N
A R A B   B E T T E   M E L D
R A D I O B R O A D C A S T
    B U Y   W E A N
W I D E S P R E A D P A N I C
H O O   T I O N     S C A L A
E N E S   N O V E L   S O L I
L I R A S   O E I L   M G R
M A R T I A N I N V A S I O N
    I N F O   E G O
  W A R O F T H E W O R L D S
H O P I   E N A T E   R O O K
Q U I Z   C O R A L   E G G Y
S K E E   T W I L L   L O S E
```

71

```
H A R L E M   A L L   A S E S
I H E A R A   F Y I   V A N E
J A D I N G   A S L   A H I T
  C R I M I N O L O G I S T
H E H   E A N   L I V A B L E
A X I S   S S S   P U R S E R
D I N A H   I W O U L D
  T A L E N T E D T E N T H
    T R O U P E   S E A M Y
P A S S E S   T S R   R K O S
I D A H O E S   S I P   E S L
P A N A F R I C A N I S M
E Y C K   I C Y   S L E E P S
I T H E   N E S   E A R T H Y
N O O R   G M T   D U B O I S
```

72

```
C H A T U P   S C O T   T B A
P E L O S I   M A T H   I O N
L I F E S C I E N C E   N O T
  R A T   A R E A   T U S K S
    A O N E   A M U S E
  L I G H T N I N G B O L T S
L A M   S E E N   T E U T O N
A R I A     S T D     R O B O
P U T N A M   O N C E   W E B
D E A D M A N W A L K I N G
    T O I L E   L O G S
M O I R A   E R A S   O O H
R H O   B O D Y B U I L D E R
E I N   L A T E   R A D I A L
D O S   E R O S   E M E N D S
```

166

73

```
F I N A L E ▪ D A M P ▪ Q U E
A M O R A L ▪ E M M A ▪ U S C
C A T C H E L E V E N ▪ I D O
E X E S ▪ C I T E ▪ A Z A N ▪
▪ ▪ ▪ I N T L ▪ T M A C ▪ ▪ ▪
▪ T E N Y E A R S A F T E R ▪
O R L ▪ T E C H ▪ I F I M A Y
H E I D I ▪ S I M ▪ L I M I T
E N Z Y M E ▪ N O S E ▪ E N D
▪ T A L E O F O N E C I T Y ▪
▪ ▪ ▪ A S E A ▪ A N K A ▪ ▪ ▪
J O H N ▪ T A C T ▪ M P E G ▪
A P U ▪ H A L F O F F S A L E
N A G ▪ O K I E ▪ O R A C L E
E L O ▪ T A P E ▪ R A M S E S
```

74

```
H E L M ▪ S T E A M ▪ A Q U A
A M E R ▪ T E S L A ▪ G U A M
J U S T P E A C E T H E O R Y
▪ ▪ S O Y A ▪ E X T E R N ▪ ▪
D O T A R D S ▪ I E S ▪ S F O
A C A D E M I C S L A V E R Y
G D R ▪ ▪ A N O ▪ ▪ I O T A S
▪ ▪ ▪ V A N G U A R D S ▪ ▪ ▪
W I P E R ▪ ▪ G R E ▪ ▪ K O A
S T R E N G T H I S B L I S S
J O Y ▪ E L I ▪ E T O I L E S
▪ ▪ ▪ I S S U E R ▪ A L B A ▪
M I N I S T R Y O F T R U T H
A N T Z ▪ E R A O F ▪ A E R O
O B O E ▪ N A N O S ▪ S A Y S
```

75

```
W A K E S ▪ H I R E ▪ S N O B
E X E R T ▪ A R A T ▪ L O N I
S E E T O ▪ M A T T ▪ A S S T
▪ P E O P L E S A Y T H A T ▪
A L S ▪ L I E ▪ N S A ▪ O L E
L I F E I S T H E ▪ L O W E R
P R I V E T ▪ U S H E R ▪ ▪ ▪
S E T I ▪ O W N T O ▪ A Y E S
▪ ▪ L I L A C ▪ R E L O C K ▪
A M I S S ▪ T H I N G B U T I
P E G ▪ L G E ▪ N E O ▪ N O M
P R E F E R R E A D I N G ▪ ▪
L I T E ▪ E M A J ▪ S O I L S
E N I D ▪ C A S A ▪ T V S E T
S O T S ▪ O N Y M ▪ S A H E L
```